She Shall Crush Thy Head
Selected Writings of St. Maximilian Kolbe

She Shall Crush Thy Head
Selected Writings of St. Maximilian Kolbe

*selected, complied, arranged,
translated and edited from the
"Pisma sw. Maksymiliana Kolbego" by*

Hilda Elfleda Brown

LEONINE PUBLISHERS
PHOENIX, ARIZONA

Copyright © 2015 Hilda Elfleda Brown

All rights reserved. No part of this book may be reproduced or transmitted in any form or by any means, electronic or mechanical, including photocopying, recording, or by any information storage or retrieval system now existing or to be invented, without written permission from the respective copyright holder(s), except for the inclusion of brief quotations in a review.

All images and sources for the author's translation were taken from public domain records, sourced online. For a complete list of these sources, readers may contact the publisher.

Published by Leonine Publishers LLC
Phoenix, Arizona
USA

ISBN-13: 978-1-942190-19-6

Library of Congress Control Number: 2015955702

Printed in the United States of America
10 9 8 7 6 5 4 3 2 1

Visit us online at www.leoninepublishers.com
For more information: info@leoninepublishers.com

St. Maximilian Kolbe,
pray for us.

Contents

Notes, Memoirs

1. Spiritual Exercises in 1917 3
2. Meditations. 3
3. Regulamentum Vitae [Rule of Life] 4
4. "Patroness of All Missions" 6
5. Lack of Confidence 8
6. Why? 10

Letters

7. To Br. Alphonse Kolbe. 12
8. To Br. Alphonse Kolbe. 12
9. To Br. Alphonse Kolbe. 13
10. To Br. Alphonse Kolbe 14
11. To Jan Pawlak 15
12. To *KI* Reader X from Zawiercie 16
13. To MI Franciscan Clerics, in Kraków. 17
14. To Fr. Alphonse Kolbe 17
15. To Fr. Alphonse Kolbe 17
16. To the III and IV Degree Teachers' School in Wirow. 18
17. To Fr. Alphonse Kolbe 19
18. To the MI headquarters in Niepokalanów . . . 19
19. To the Cleric Bernardo Hatada. 20

20. To Niepokalanów 20
21. To Niepokalanów 21
22. To the Cleric Br. Alexander Żuchowski 25

Manuscripts

23. MI 28
24. Catholic Action 28
25. Today's Enemies of the Church 34
26. The Archconfraternity of the Holy Rosary . . 39
27. The Rosary. 41
28. MI 42
29. [Directive for the *Small Daily*] 43

Articles

30. From the Editor 48
31. Where Is Happiness?. 48
32. Greatness and Sanctity 50
33. Goal of the MI 53
34. The First Condition 53
35. God's Grace and the Saints' Natural Gifts. . . 54
36. The First Nativity Play and the First
    Shepherd's Mass. 58
37. Threatening Danger 60
38. Does God Exist?. 62
39. The Church and Socialism 66
40. Who Is God? 70
41. The Lenten Fast 72

42. The Blessed Virgin Mary's Mediation 74
43. November 27. 76
44. Without "Clearer Proofs". 78
45. About the Militia of the Immaculata. 80
46. The Immaculata's Orders 83
47. Why Do the Good Suffer? 86
48. I Am an Unbeliever 87
49. Does Truth Change? 88
50. Body of the Lord 90
51. Papal Infallibility. 92
52. Victory of the Immaculata 94
53. Does Almighty God Know Everything?. 96
54. The Cult of the Immaculate Conception . . . 99
55. "Knight of the Immaculata" 105
56. The Same Old Thing 106
57. How Should a Knight (or Lady) of the Immaculata Think and Act?. 108
58. Queen of Poland 110
59. To the Most Sacred Heart of Jesus through the Immaculata 113
60. The Carmelite Scapular 116
61. The Secret of Strength and Power 119
62. On the Rosary.... 122
63. More Thinking! 125
64. From the Publisher. 127
65. The Latest Fashion 128
66. Penance, Penance, Penance... 129
67. Heaven 132

- 68. Miracles 135
- 69. When Will It Come to Pass?... 137
- 70. Our Power 139
- 71. Hell 141
- 72. Why?... 142
- 73. Our War 143
- 74. The Month of May 146
- 75. Visit of Mrs. Kawai, the wife of the minister plenipotentiary, in Niepokalanów 147
- 76. Knowledge 149
- 77. Memories of the Past Four Years 150
- 78. How We Come to Know God 152
- 79. If God Were to Cease to Exist... 153
- 80. Faith 155
- 81. Prayer 156
- 82. Our Ideal 159
- 83. MI 161
- 84. On the Second Day of July 163
- 85. What We Can Do 164
- 86. The Lord Is Truly Risen! 167
- 87. Where Are We Going? 168

Notes, Memoirs

Marie

Kto kocha Niepokalaną tem ofiarniej ten się zbawi, uświęci i innych do uświęcenia doprowadzi.

br M Maksymilian Kse

1. Spiritual Exercises in 1917

[Retreat, Rome, 23 X 1917]

I

Love crosses. The cross, the cross, the cross = source of genuine happiness.

II

<u>Patience</u>. Look down to hell, into heaven, and on the cross. The degree of glory in heaven depends on the degree of patience.

III

<u>Confirmation</u>. Liberalism (denies the supernatural), modernism (*non serviam*) [I will not serve]. Wants to adapt to the times in a human way. "Praised be Jesus Christ."

2. Meditations

[Meditations, Rome, 11 II 1918]

<u>February</u>

11—(Thoughts). Leave everyone and everything and follow Our Lord Jesus. Prayer. *Non conturbatione Dominus* [the Lord is not in confusion] et al.

(From a conference at 6 pm). <u>Characteristics</u> of the supernatural life: "I am the Immaculate Conception," 1) value and desire only the supernatural, Almighty God; 2) pray for sinners, <u>hatred of sin</u>, "penance, penance, penance"—mortified life; 3) do not pamper the body; 4) Blessed Virgin Mary <u>always</u> appeared with rosary. Prayer. Naturalism is the plague, the wound of our century.

3. Regulamentum Vitae [Rule of Life]

[Retreat, Kraków, February 1920]

1) I must be the greatest saint.

2) The <u>greatest</u> glory of God through the salvation and most perfect sanctification of myself and of all, who are and who will be, through the Immaculata—MI3.

3) *Peccatum mortale vel veniale deliberatum a priori exclude* [from the very outset exclude mortal sin and deliberate venial sin]. Serenity about the past. With ardor make up for lost time.

4) I will not leave a) <u>any evil</u> without making reparation for it (destroy it) and b) <u>any good</u> undone, that I can perform, increase, or contribute to it in any way.

5) *Regula tua oboedientia* [your rule is obedience] = God's will through the Immaculata.
Instrument.

6) <u>Do what you are doing</u>; do not pay attention to anything else, good or bad.

7) *Semper quieta, amorosa actio* [always peaceful, loving action].

8) *Serva ordinem, et ordo servabit te* [preserve order, and order will preserve you].

9) *Praeparatio, actio, conclusio* [preparation, action, conclusion].

10) Remember always, that you are the **Immaculata's** <u>thing and property</u> in an absolute, unconditional, <u>unlimited</u>, <u>irrevocable</u> way:

whatever you are, whatever you have or can do, all your *actiones* (thought, word, deed) and *passiones* (pleasant, unpleasant, indifferent) are totally Her property. Let it therefore be done with all this, whatever pleases Her (and not you). Likewise all your intentions are Hers: therefore, may She change, add, subtract them as it pleases Her (since She cannot violate justice).

You are an **instrument** in Her hands, therefore do only that which She wishes: accept everything from Her hands. Have recourse to Her in all things **like a child** to his mother; entrust everything to Her.

Seek for **Her**, for **Her veneration**, for **Her affairs**, yet leave the care of yourself and your people to Her.

Nothing from yourself, but acknowledge all as received **from Her**.

The entire fruit of your work depends on your union with Her, just as She is the instrument of divine mercy.

Life (each of its instants), death (where, when, and how) and my eternity, it is all **Yours, O Immaculata**. Do with it all **whatever** pleases **You**.

11) *Omnia possum in Eo, qui me per Immaculatam confortat* [I can do all things in Him, who strengthens me through the Immaculata].

12) Interior life: *totus primo sibi et sic totus omnibus* [first entirely to yourself and thus entirely to all] [...].

4. "Patroness of All Missions" [1]

[Memoir, Mugenzai no Sono, after 25 VII 1932]

Maria

Such is the title Holy Church gave to the recently deceased St. Thérèse of the Child Jesus. In fact, it is not just a title; after my journey from Japan to India and back, I'm personally convinced that there is not one place where she is not particularly honored. There is not a church where you do not see her; rather, the little saint immediately comes to your eyes in a painting or figure, or very often in a separate altar dedicated to her. There is no lack, either, of new magnificent churches built in her name and, let's say forthrightly, for her interest, because truly dropping from heaven, as promised, is a torrential rain of roses of diverse graces. She stirs up generosity for the construction of these churches.

Should I also tell of my "dealings" with her? Well, even before her beatification and canonization, while reading a biography of her, I said to her, "I will make a memento (remembrance in prayer) in every Holy Mass for your beatification and canonization, and you will take care of my mission."

While preparing the first missionary expedition to the Far East, when she had already been beatified and canonized, I stopped by Lisieux and presented myself at the gate of the convent where she sanctified herself, and where her three sisters still reside, to tell a sister of St. Thérèse to inform her holy sister that I have pretensions against her, because a pact was made, and now she was already canonized, while where was my mission?... And shortly I found myself in Japan.

And also recently in India, where I had the task of looking around for a new Niepokalanów, so many difficulties accumulated, that I had lost all hope for a favorable resolution of the matter. So, standing once before a statue of St. Thérèse, placed on a shelf, at the foot of which was lying a bouquet of large flowers like roses, I prayed with a certain "grief" and concluded, "Let's see if you remember." At that moment, one of the flowers fell on the table under the statue. This made a strange impression on me, yet I thought to myself, "We'll see what that means." From that moment, unexpectedly, all the difficulties, without any intervention on my part, completely disappeared, and the matter was resolved beyond all expectations, because I received there right away for the use of Niepokalanów the land for the expansion, a sizable chapel, and a building completely sufficient for starting publication of the *Knight* in Indian (Malayan).

Whence comes such "competence" in missionary matters? Did she perhaps, in life, do missionary work in many pagan countries? Did she shed her blood as a martyr? None of this. She never even crossed the threshold of her cloister in Lisieux, France. In her life she wrought no miracles, but in ordinary, everyday grim life, she sanctified herself so much. For it is not a question of what we do, but <u>how</u> we do it—with what intention and how much love.

And what was her intention? To give pleasure to the Lord Jesus, the Infant Jesus. This is pure love. To daily carry crosses with love, to work with love, to live for love, to be a little child who with caresses of love takes hold of its father's and mother's heart.

Such a missionary everyone can and must be.

Yet how to attain it?

St. Thérèse called herself "the Immaculata's little flower" and admits that the Immaculata brought her up. Let us also be Her little flowers, and She will teach us limitless confidence in God's merciful love, of which She is the personification [2].

[1] Publish in the Polish, Japanese, Italian *Knight*?
[2] In the Polish *Knight* publish the photograph of St. Thérèse in Niepokalanów.

5. Lack of Confidence

[Memoir, Mugenzai no Sono, 1932–1933]

Maria!

Sometimes life is so hard. It seems that there is no exit. The wall cannot be broken with one's head. And life is sad, and hard, and at times terrible, and desperate.

But why?

Is it really so awful to live in the world?

Doesn't Almighty God know everything? Isn't He all powerful? Are not all of nature's laws, and even all men's hearts, in His hands? Could anything happen in the universe, that He does not permit?... And if He permits it, could He permit something that would not be for our own good, for our greater good, in fact, our greatest good?...

And if for a moment we were given infinite intelligence and understood all the causes and effects, we would not choose anything other than what Almighty God allows for us, because as He is infinitely wise, He knows best what is better for our soul, and as He is infinitely good, He wants and permits only what will lead to our greater happiness in heaven.

Why is it, then, that we are sometimes so desperate?

Because we do not see the relationship between our happiness and these circumstances that trouble us, and further, on account of the narrowness of our heads (which can fit into a hat), <u>we cannot</u> know everything.

So what should we do?

Trust in God. Through that confidence, without understanding things directly, we give even greater glory to God, because we acknowledge His wisdom, goodness, and power.

Therefore, let us trust in God, and let us trust in Him without limit. Let us be confident that if we only seek to fulfill His will, nothing truly evil can happen to us, even if we were living in an age that is a thousand times more difficult.

Should we, then, not attempt to avoid or overcome difficulties?

Certainly, we can and must do this. Insofar as it depends on us alone, we should do all we can to remove difficulties in our life's path, but without anxiety, without grim sadness, and above all without desperate hopelessness. These states of soul do not help to resolve the problems, and furthermore they make us incapable of wise, prudent, and quick foresight.

In everything, let us not forget to repeat with Our Lord Jesus in the garden of Gethsemane, "But yet not my will, but Thy will be done." And when Almighty God should consider it appropriate, as in Gethsemane, to not fulfill our request but rather to send us a chalice to drink to the dregs, let us not forget that Our Lord Jesus not only suffered but after suffering also rose gloriously from the dead. And that we, too, through suffering tend toward the resurrection.

Furthermore, we get too attached to this wretched world; what would happen if from time to time no thorn would prick us? Perhaps then we would want to set up heaven right here in the midst of this earthly dust and mud.

Therefore, let us trust in Almighty God through the Immaculata with a boundless trust, and let us strive to the extent of our understanding and strength to do something about it—but peacefully, placing our faith in the Immaculata, and God's will always above our own. Then crosses will become for us, as they should be, the rungs whereby we climb toward the happiness of our resurrection in heaven.

M. K.

6. Why?

[Memoir, Mugenzai no Sono, 1932–1933]

Maria!

I've known young men who very much loved the Immaculata our common Mother, but later...they went astray.

Why?

Perhaps the Immaculata Herself drew them away from Her?

No, never, never.

So then what happened?

We always have our free will, and neither God nor the Immaculata will force our will. Therefore, if we want to, we can at any time abandon God, abandon the Immaculata. We can—condemn ourselves forever. If we want to.

What a terrifying truth. And still, if we did not have free will, there would be no merit, no reward, no heaven.

St. Alphonsus shuddered at the thought of whether he would persevere to the end [...].

I've noticed that the devil first of all tries to deprive his victim of the Immaculata's Miraculous Medal, with whatever pretense, and then it goes easier for him.

Letters

7. To Br. Alphonse Kolbe

[Kraków, 9 VIII 1920]

[...] I received a letter with a poem; beautiful is the way, the true royal way (of the cross), leading directly to heaven. Love is inflamed after these thorns. [...]

8. To Br. Alphonse Kolbe

[Zakopane, 4 X 1920]

Praised Be Jesus Christ

Dear Brother,
[...] If you fulfill that which you proposed in it, you will soon be a saint. But it is a road to the infinite; and it, itself, is infinite. Hence, *qui sanctus est sanctificetur adhuc* [he that is holy, let him be sanctified still"]; and the one who engages himself further on this road more clearly recognizes how much remains to be traveled, and how little it is which he has undergone, in comparison to the whole. The faster he runs, the more he recognizes the slowness of his current pace. So it is ever beginning anew, without stop, and our holy father Francis on his deathbed said, "Let us begin to do good." [...]

An incompetent answer, and sometimes silence becomes the seed of indifference, if not disbelief. [...]

Fr. Maximilian M. Kolbe

9. To Br. Alphonse Kolbe

[Zakopane, 27 X 1920]

[...] Reason is above the senses, and faith is above reason, although faith is, *"rationabile" obsequium, quoad evidentiam extrinsecam, non autem intrinsecam* [a compliance "of reason" in regards to the extrinsic evidence but not the intrinsic]. And the more reason does not see the *evidentiam intrinsecam* [the intrinsic evidence] and yet follows faith, the greater is the glory it gives to God by acknowledging His infinite wisdom, goodness, and power. Perfection consists in the love of God, in being united with Him, divinization. Love reveals itself through the realization of God's will, which is revealed to us through the superiors' will, if this isn't openly and certainly contrary to God's law (*explicite vel implicite*) [explicitly or implicitly]; in fact, there exists also a subordination of laws and superiors to God's law. The Guardian Angel of [St.] Gemma [Galgani] told her that the shortest and most genuine road to heaven is obedience.

Abandonment to the will of God and its fulfillment, especially in things contrary to the senses and even to a limited and fallible reason, inflames the love of God. The cross is a school of love.

Wishing, that the Immaculata won't spare Her "Militia" crosses and each of the members because of Her, for thus their intentions will be purified, so that they do not accede to Her nor in Her, will work for show or internal satisfaction, but out of pure love [...].

Let the members work together to strive to know well the present antireligious currents—the principles of [erroneous] belief, socialism, Bolshevism, masonry, Protestantism, etc.—and learn how to counteract them.

[...] I think that the MI [Militia Immaculatae] should remain on a road, arduous and harsh, but advantageous in the work of coming to know errors, prejudices, antireligious sentiments, which are spread so widely today—their nature, the creation of their detrimental consequences, methods of propaganda, their representatives and how to counteract them, how to save as many lost souls as possible, and not turn into a literary or artistic association, because it would then fail in its purpose. [...]

From my own experience, I know that this isn't the same as learning something for academic purposes, to be prepared for anyone from any sphere of society, so as to present an issue in order to convince him. Therefore, let God keep that MI member, being anywhere, in company or on the train, from needing to dismiss some objection against religion with an evasive answer, thereby weakening the faith of his listeners. And such incidents have happened, and even among priests.

10. To Br. Alphonse Kolbe

[Zakopane, 8 XII 1920]

[...] As for the MI, it is understood that we are instruments in the Immaculata's hands, so we must act only as much as She wishes (and this is demonstrated through obedience). And I now limit myself to the activities of a simple member, and in a rather limited way, because She so wishes. The Immaculate has allowed me to approach the academics living here in the Brotherly Help nursing home. They have an irreligious reputation, and not without reason. The socialist (so they say) administration is composed of who knows what sort of leaders. Now, they (i.e., a selected circle of patients and academics) have invited me and with much insistence, that I might explain to them some religious issues. So I arranged a series of apologetic talks, in which each of them could freely take the floor. We passed from the existence of God to the divinity of Christ Our Lord. They even purchased Szczepanski's "New Testament," "Evenings on Lake Leman," and Bartynowski's "Apologetics." [...]

Let us be careful that we not do in the MI more than what obedience permits, because then we would no longer act as instruments in the Immaculata's hands. [...]

If you could, please find the song to the Virgin Mary "J'irai la voir un jour; Au ciel a ma patrie; J'irai voir Marie; Ma joie et mon amour. (bis) Au ciel, au ciel, au ciel; J'irai, la voir un jour," but in the Polish language, along with the music (for one voice). In Italy, we sang it in French, it is beautiful. One of the novices told me that he heard it in a nuns' church (?) in Vilnius (in Polish) and...he wept with emotion. If, therefore, you can find it, please do send it to me. [...]

11. To Jan Pawlak

[Grodno, 22 III 1924]

[...] As for the activity program, previous experience has taught me not to restrict too much with rules and little rules, but rather to give more spontaneity to plans and intentions. Above all, union with the Immaculata's will is the secret of success, and therefore prayer—humble, trusting, and loving prayer—infuses light into the intellect and gives fortitude to the will. The Immaculate Herself removes impediments. It seems to me that in regard to the reading room, it perhaps would be better if some lad or some lady were on call, whereas the members of the Militia should be the soul of everything, but externally as the least visible. Let no one know them. Thus it will be possible to penetrate into many places where openly the entrance would be completely closed.

With the Immaculata's help we must endeavor that faithful Knights of the Immaculata be found everywhere, and especially in such important fields as 1) youth education (professors of educational institutions, teachers, sports associations); 2) media management (magazines, newspapers, editing and distribution thereof, public rentals, lending libraries, etc., lectures, films, cinema, etc.); 3) fine arts (sculpture, painting, music, theater); and finally 4) let our MI become in every field the first pioneers and leaders in the sciences (natural history, history, literature, medicine, law, physical sciences, etc.). Under our influence and the MI's care, may industrial and commercial facilities, banks, etc. rise and flourish.

In a word, may the Militia permeate everything and in a common spirit heal, strengthen, and develop everything for the greater glory of God through the Immaculata and for the good of mankind. [...]

12. To *KI* Reader X from Zawiercie

[Grodno, 12 IX 1924]

[...] Please do not be discouraged because indifference and malice prevail, for God's grace through the Immaculate is stronger. [...]

The goal of the Militia of the Immaculata is to conquer the whole world, all hearts and each individually for the Queen not only of heaven but also of earth and to give true happiness to those poor unhappy men who seek it in the passing pleasures of this world—this indeed is our goal.

You must win Zawiercie for the Immaculata; here is your outpost. You must fight with prayers, good example, and kindness, a great sweetness and kindness as a reflection of the Immaculata's goodness. Those people who seek happiness outside of God are unhappy—entangled in sins and defects, they pursue happiness and seek it where it cannot be found, seek it where it simply is not.

Also, may the Immaculata's Miraculous Medal be the weapon, or rather the bullet, that is used by every Knight of the Immaculata. Even if someone is of the worst sort, if only he agrees to wear the Miraculous Medal, give it to him [...] and pray for him, and occasionally with a kind word, seek to slowly bring him to wholeheartedly love the Immaculate Mother and to have recourse to Her in all difficulties and temptations. He who sincerely begins to pray to the Immaculata will soon, especially on Her feast, be persuaded to go to confession. There is much evil in the world, but let us remember that the Immaculata is more powerful and that "She shall crush the infernal serpent's head." [...]

13. To MI Franciscan Clerics, in Kraków

[Grodno, 1 IV 1925]

[...] The period of the present work is a time of preparation for the future fight under the Immaculata's banner. This task is highly significant and is difficult. In this your work you must pay attention, above all, to your interior life. In vain would you exercise your mind, in vain would you fill your head with manifold beautiful and necessary notions, if you lacked this inner filial relationship with the Immaculata as our Mother, Queen, Commander, and Hope. [...]

14. To Fr. Alphonse Kolbe

[Zakopane, 29 IX 1926]

[...] The ideals of the MI and of the "Knight" [are] through the veneration of the Immaculata to rectify morality and through articles to deepen adequately the knowledge of religion, contrary to the resolution of the Freemasons. [...]

15. To Fr. Alphonse Kolbe

[Zakopane, 12 X 1926]

[...] Our goal: to conquer every soul for the Immaculata, and the justness of our goal: because Freemasonry has resolved that "we will not conquer the Catholic religion by reasoning, only by the corruption of morals," which is cleverly executed by way of literature, art, theater, cinema, fashion, etc., yet from history it can be ascertained that those who love the Immaculata do not fall into the mire, or if they fall, they arise quickly; all conversions originate from this Mediatrix of all graces. [...]

16. To the III and IV Degree Teachers' School in Wirow

[Zakopane, before 6 III 1927]

[...] At one of its conventions Freemasonry resolved, "We will not conquer the Catholic religion by reasoning, only by the corruption of morals"—what a clever resolution!

In its first part, it testifies to the truth of the Catholic religion, for the truth cannot be overcome by reasoning—indeed it then becomes even more apparent. In the second part it truly hits the weak point, for when someone wades into moral mire, for him religion is something inconvenient; he does not want to think about it and proclaims everywhere that he does not believe in God, as though someone has already proved that there is no God.

Yet for him, Almighty God is inconvenient, for he does not conceive of that higher happiness which alone can fill and satisfy the great spirit of man.

St. Paul long ago wrote, "An unbelieving man does not understand this," and Our Lord Jesus Himself taught, "Blessed are the pure in heart, for they shall see God"—obviously in this world—with the eyes of faith.

Clever, therefore, was this resolution, and pursuant to it they purposely and systematically began to defile literature, art, theater, cinema, fashion, etc. And if before there remained much to be desired, afterward immorality began to gush forth from all possible sources and flood our cities and even villages, dragging behind it a weakening of the faith in accordance with the correct predictions of the resolution.

The Immaculata—of whom it was said, "She shall crush thy head," i.e., of the infernal serpent—shall crush also this head of Freemasonry, which directs all of the antireligious and immoral movements and provides large amounts of money for the formation of new sects.

Let us totally give ourselves to Her, so that She deigns to use us as instruments for the salvation and sanctification of souls. Let us conquer hearts for Her, because wherever She enters, there also enters divine grace, and from it comes salvation and sanctification. [...]

17. To Fr. Alphonse Kolbe

[Nagasaki, 2 IX 1930]

[...] Look through the book of Bl. Grignion de Montfort *On True Devotion to the Blessed Virgin Mary*, a little bit every day, because it is truly something that is "ours."

18. To the MI headquarters in Niepokalanów

[Nagasaki, 11 IV 1932]

[...] Now we already have the proper Office, Holy Mass, and liturgical feast of the Mother of God Mediatrix of All Graces; Cardinal Mercier sought very diligently for the proclamation of this truth as a dogma. Perhaps the Immaculata will allow us to contribute to the setting of this gem in Her crown.

19. To the Cleric Bernardo Hatada

[Kobe, 30 V 1932]

Maria!

My Dear Sir,
[...] If it is permitted me to add something more, I would propose two things: 1) obedience, which is the easiest, shortest, and surest way to sanctity, and furthermore a supernatural obedience, union of our will with God's will, constitutes the very essence of sanctity, namely, perfect charity; and 2) filial love, devotion to the Blessed Virgin Mary. She will teach you perfect supernatural obedience. She will obtain and give you strength to proceed on this road, and even as the best mother she will bear you securely in Her arms, pressing you lovingly to Her Immaculate Heart during the most difficult portions of this journey. These are merely some imperfect words, but you will understand much more from personal experience.

Always your brother in the Immaculata's Heart
Maximilian M. Kolbe

20. To Niepokalanów

[Mugenzai no Sono, 11 II 1933]

In the month of May, we celebrated the second anniversary of our arrival in Nagasaki. At dinner, there was sitting beside me Amaki, a young man who was converted by us. We remembered how the Immaculata guided us and established us in Japanese soil and in Nagasaki.

Among other things, the young man expressed himself like this: "*Anata gata kimasen deshitara, watakushi wa mata shinja ni naranakatta desho*"—that is, "If you had not come here, I would still be a pagan."

There was so much sincerity and gratitude in these words toward the Immaculata and to us, Her instruments, that involuntarily the thought came to my mind: even if no one else converted, besides this one, it would have been worthwhile to undertake these hardships and still to sacrifice much, much more—for after all, here is a soul.

But through the intercession of the Immaculata two more persons were baptized at the same time after that first baptism. And very recently there were another three, while a fourth, after having prepared with us, received the grace of holy baptism at Osaka. Besides this, there are many letters that proclaim the Immaculata's powerful work in souls; we only regret that we are not able to purchase more machines and paper to further distribute the *Knight of the Immaculata*.

Glory to the Immaculata for all that She has accomplished, is accomplishing, and will continue to accomplish.

Rycerz Niepokalanej

21. To Niepokalanów

[On the Indian Ocean, between Bombay and Colombo, en route to the Japanese Niepokalanów, 22 IX 1933.
Published with some changes in RN 12 (1933) pp. 559–562]

Maria

The Immaculata gains the noble heart of a Japanese person in Warsaw.

When I arrived from Japan to the Polish Niepokalanów, I learned that, in Warsaw, the wife of the Japanese minister plenipotentiary, Mrs. Kawai, is a Catholic, and his children are also baptized according to the rites of the Catholic Church. So I sent Mrs. Kawai a statue of the Immaculata. In response, she invited me to Skolimow, a villa on the outskirts of Warsaw, where she spent the summer with her children. So I went there with Fr. Florian Koziurą, the present guardian of Niepokalanów. When we entered the parlor, we were pleasantly surprised at the sight of the statue of the Immaculata that I sent earlier; it was set amidst of flowers, gazing at all of us. She therefore already lovingly reigns there.

The conversation turned to the minister's illness, who was hospitalized for a lung ailment at Otwock, and to Niepokalanów and the Polish and Japanese, and this and that. In the end, Mrs. Kawai declares that she has a request.

—Gladly - I answer.

—I would like to confess, and one of my servants, too. And another request.

—With the greatest pleasure.

—My mother is thinking about being baptized.

—I have not yet written to Japan - pointed out Mrs. Narahara.

I then explained that it is too serious and too personal a matter to be decided by others.

—I have one more request - adds the minister's wife.

—Please go ahead; I live only for souls, that is my task.

—At Otwock the minister is assisted by a Japanese lady who is studying the catechism and also desires baptism. Perhaps you, Father, could go there?

We therefore arranged the preparations, although briefly, for the mother's baptism and the trip to Otwock.

—And something else: my ten-year-old elder daughter has not yet received First Holy Communion, and it is difficult for her to learn the truths of the Faith from a catechism in French.

On the appointed day a car, carrying the minister's wife, her mother, and me, sped along the road to Otwock. On the way, I learned that the minister is indeed a pagan, though he not only has permitted the baptism of his children but also has been in contact with the Jesuits and is well disposed toward religion.

And so, I went to him and we conversed about religion. He readily understood that truth is only one, and hence true religion can only be one. That God, too, is only One. But when it came to the Holy Trinity—he pointed out that the Chinese also have similar beliefs. I willingly admitted that many truths more or less distorted and blurred can be seen in the various creeds around the world.

His wife gave him the Immaculata's Miraculous Medal, a few of which I had given her, both for the minister and for his entire family. He accepted it and placed it on a small table.

He showed me also a book in French, [entitled] *Jesus Christ*, and said that, however, he still was not convinced. He also spoke of his impressions from his stay at Lourdes, but these also were not enough.

The illness was by now visibly leading him to the grave, and his emaciated face and faded hands foretold the end.

We returned and arranged for the baptism of Mrs. Narahara—after she had some more preparation—on the feast of the Assumption at Niepokalanów, and of the servant, a little later, for she still lacked some elementary knowledge.

On the eve of the baptism, however, the minister's health had so greatly worsened that his whole family had to rush to his bedside, and it was necessary to postpone the matter of the baptism. I had also received an invitation to go to Otwock. I left the Japanese embassy, along with Mr. Hirata, the current *chargé d'affaires*, a Japanese doctor, Misawa, from Berlin, and Dr. Rudzki from Warsaw. I asked Dr. Rudzki if he would, after his examination of the sick man, openly reveal to me his condition, because it was related to his baptism.

—What you should do, Father, do it right away, because the patient will die today—was the sound judgment of Dr. Rudzki at Otwock.

In the meantime, I also notified the apostolic nuncio Msgr. Marmaggi. I had heard previously that he was to return from vacation after the feast of the Assumption, but something had caused him to go earlier to the capital, and so a phone call found him at home. He promised to come soon. I decided, therefore, to wait for his arrival. When he showed up in the corridor, I recounted to him everything. So he went to the sick man. He reminded him of their old friendship and presented to him the fundamental truths of the Faith. Meanwhile, outside, his wife and her mother, and two priests—the nuncio's secretary and I—were praying for him, individually and in silence.

The grace of faith descended into the noble heart of the minister. To a question asked—after some explanations—he replied,

—I believe. I believe.

—And do you want to be baptized?

—I do.

The Rev. Nuncio poured water on the sick man's head, saying,

—Francis, I baptize you in the name of the Father and of the Son and of the Holy Spirit.

After holy baptism—as testified to by those who were around him—a great joy entered the heart of the minister. His soul, a few hours after holy baptism, pure as an angel, was taken by the Immaculata to heaven, on the vigil of Her assumption.

When his body was temporarily laid in the mortuary at the Powązki cemetery, every day, in the Japanese legation, the minister's children and the mother of the minister's wife and the servant gathered for catechism in Japanese, so that on the vigil of the Nativity of Our Lady, those not baptized were reborn in the water of baptism, and on the very day of the feast, the children and the newly baptized, for the first time, received Holy Communion, and all of them received the sacrament of confirmation from the hands of His Excellency the Rev. Nuncio, in the nunciature chapel. [...]

Fr. Maximilian M. Kolbe

22. To the Cleric Br. Alexander Żuchowski

[Niepokalanów, 25 IX 1940]

I do not have here at hand a Marian bibliography, and even our library is only in the early stages, and therefore it is difficult for me to specify the titles of the needed books.

[...] Cardinal Mercier's extensive pastoral letter, *On the universal mediation of the Blessed Virgin Mary*, translated by Fr. Jacek Woroniecki and published by the Pallottines. [...]

I do not have anything more to send you. Anyways, this issue one penetrates more deeply with one's knees than with one's brain. [...]

Manuscripts

23. MI

[Autograph Manuscript, Kraków, before 18 IX 1919]

[...] At various times the Blessed Virgin Mary has come to the aid of Her children and has given them different ways of more easily attaining salvation and of liberating others from Satan's yoke. Now, in the age of the Immaculate Conception, the Blessed Virgin has given mankind the Miraculous Medal, the heavenly origin of which has been confirmed by countless miracles of healing and particularly of conversion. The Immaculata Herself, in revealing it, promised to all who would wear it very many graces; because conversion is a divine grace, the Miraculous Medal is the best means of attaining our goal. Therefore, it constitutes a first-class weapon of the Militia; it is the bullet with which a faithful *Miles* [Knight] strikes at the enemy, i.e., evil, thereby saving those who have fallen into evil. "***Et praesertim Numisma Miraculosum***" ["And above all the Miraculous Medal"]. [...]

24. Catholic Action

[Autograph Manuscript, Kraków, 1919]

MI

This subject is too extensive for me to be able to thoroughly exhaust it in this paper. Therefore, I will omit the most important—though, alas, unappreciated, in our times—division of Catholic Action, i.e., prayer and the great significance of the contemplative orders. I will also leave out the activity of suffering and penance. I don't intend to speak here even of good example, though "*exempla* [examples] precisely *trahunt* [attract]." I will limit myself only to the action of the word and, especially, of the printed word—the press.

For indeed, truthfully Napoleon said, a hundred years ago, when not many yet knew how to read, that "the press is the fifth power of the world." The Jews understood that immediately; let me say it more clearly—the **Masons**, who with iron consistency are endeavoring to realize the motto adopted in 1717: "to destroy all religion, especially Christianity." The French Jew Cremieux, founder of a worldwide Jewish association, at a Congress of Masons did not hesitate, even sixty years ago, to say, "Hold everything as nothing, money as nothing, esteem as nothing, the press is everything. Having the press, we will have everything." And at an international Congress of Rabbis in Kraków in 1848, the English rabbi Moses Montefiore proclaimed, "As long as the newspapers of the world are not in our hands, all will be useless. Let us be mindful of the eleventh commandment: ***Thou shalt not suffer*** *over yourself any foreign press, so that you rule long over the Gentiles*. Let us control the press, and soon we will rule and direct the fate of all Europe."

Pursuant to these watchwords, they intensively set to work and, unfortunately, have already accomplished a very great deal. A considerable number, if not the majority, of the most widely read daily newspapers are in their hands. Suffice it to say that in so "Catholic" an Austria, already at the beginning of this century, 360 periodicals in the German language alone fought against the Church; eighty-three of them were daily newspapers. The circulation of the bad press amounted to 2,000,000, of which 1,200,000 was accounted for by daily newspapers. Concerning Germany, the literary critic Bartels wrote that two-thirds—if not three-fourths—of the magazines and periodicals belong to Jews; in Hungary, of 1,000 periodicals, 800 are in Jewish hands. Subsequently they took control of nearly all the telegraph agencies, and through them they direct also other publications. The agency Reuters in London alone supplies 5,000 daily newspapers. The agency Stefani in Rome—all the Italian daily newspapers; the agency Havas in Paris—the French, Spanish, and Belgian; the agency Wolff in Berlin, all the German; and the agency Associated Press in New York—the American daily newspaper service.

The fatal course of the effective activity of the bad press is revealed to us by the Jesuit Fr. Abel, called the apostle of Vienna, in this classic example. Once they summoned him to a sick person. The dying person, having seen the priest, showed him a whole stack of newspapers folded up in the corner of the room and told his story: "Look, Father, that is the greatest enemy of my life. I was the son of pious parents who raised me well, so that even at the university I was a good Catholic. From the moment I became a doctor, I thought it appropriate to subscribe to a so-called periodical for the intelligentsia, namely, one of the Jewish periodicals. In the first fourteen weeks, this daily newspaper's continuous assaults on my faith angered me, but later I became indifferent, and within a year I stopped all religious practices and became an unbeliever, up to this very moment in which divine grace is restoring to me my faith." Not differently does the press act also among the common people.

Also the popular writer Wetzel rightly complains, "Look at today's world, how it has changed in recent decades! Who is sowing unbelief among the people? Who is depriving them of their hope for heaven and causing the people to seek their happiness in earthly pleasures? Who muffled the conscience in their hearts? Who broke the state laws, disturbed public order, so that more and more frequently crimes of any kind are committed?! All of that is the work of the daily press hostile to the Church. In several major European cities a whole number of overpaid scribblers daily spill all their gall at everything Catholic. Hundreds of periodicals and daily newspapers repeat the same thing, and in this manner this venom from day to day penetrates into hundreds of thousands of families, poisoning millions of souls. So works the gigantic machine of the daily press, put in the service of unbelief and bad morals." Lassalle, though himself a socialist, looking at the enormity of evil that the press has wrought, cannot refrain from condemning it: "In its deceitfulness, baseness, and immorality," he writes, "it surpasses perhaps only its own stupidity. If a change in our press does not take place, and this press continues for some fifty years in this way, it will be mad, the spirit of the people will be entirely poisoned. This is the greatest crime that I know of."

It is time and high time for a change to occur. But the first step in this change—is to utterly boycott the bad press; then—to support the good. Painful are the words of Wetzla in this regard: "The godless press would never have reached such a state of development, had not millions of Catholics supported the magazines and daily newspapers hostile to the Church and the so-called independent ones, whether with subscription or collaboration," and Fr. Kolb in the Fifth Congress of Catholics in Austria uses words that are even more severe: "What can we say about a people that pays for its own debasement? I do not find a name for it! And this infamy falls on Catholics, offended constantly by thousands of newspapers. These writings, which shamelessly scoff at Catholics, are printed for us Catholics! They do not, however, send them anonymously in the form of lampoons, but we ourselves request it and pay for it. Could we be more blind in the face of such a threatening danger? And this our blindness directly becomes a crime, since not only we do not defend ourselves against this danger, but we possess and read bad magazines—we pay for the offense to and derision of our Faith! Indeed, in us Catholics are fulfilled the words of the prophet: '*We searched as blind men for the wall, as without eyes we searched. We stumbled at noonday, as if we were in a fog, and in the dark, as dead.*'"

Bishop Zwerger (in 1884) said of such people, "Whoever gives money to the bad press is waging war against the Church and cannot be called a true Catholic," and Bishop Ketteler of Mainz goes further and says that "he who is **indifferent** in regard to the press does not have the right to be called a faithful son of the Church."

Cardinal Nagl, in 1911, writes, "It's the obligation of every Catholic to stand in defense of the Catholic press and support it with prayer, word, and deed." The archbishop of Zaragoza at the Congress of Catholic Journalists in 1910 did not hesitate to say, "There are many wealthy Catholics that use their wealth to found new churches and monasteries, or to adorn them with paintings of the saints. Undoubtedly it is a very beautiful thing! But, unfortunately, one misfortune can destroy all this, whereas the fruits of a good daily journal are simply indestructible. Would it not, therefore, be a better thing to found a large daily newspaper for the good of the people? Nowadays the daily newspaper is a rapidly firing cannon. God wills it!"

The Popes think no differently on this issue.

Already Pius IX has said, "It is the sacred obligation of every Catholic to support the press and disseminate it among the people. A good press is a **most advantageous** work that sows tremendous merit." And **Leo XIII**: "The bad press has lost the society of Christianity; one must therefore oppose it with a good press. Catholics must not cease to work for their good press, remembering that a good press is an **unceasing mission**." Speaking (on February 21, 1879) to Catholic editors, he said, "We are convinced that our times demand these very means (Catholic publications) and energetic defenders of... The revolutionary men went out of their way to spread among people a whole series of newspapers, whose main purpose is to contest principles of the truths of the Faith, calumniate the Church, and inculcate in souls pernicious convictions... Forasmuch as the publishing of newspapers is regarded as the main means of this action in modern times, therefore the principal obligation of Catholic writers is to turn this means, used by the enemies for the ruin of society and the Church, into a saving medium for the people and to use it for the purposes of defending the Church."

The Holy Father, Pius X, in 1905, wrote to the Mexican bishops, "As to the newspapers and journals, I would like, once and for all, to convince the consciously minded that they should try with all their power to ensure that Catholics hold in their hands only truly Catholic magazines and newspapers. Today this is, in my opinion, the **most important** thing."

In 1908, while speaking in an audience with clergy, he expressed himself even more strongly: "Neither the people nor the clergy have understood the importance of the press. They say that in the past the press did not exist; they do not understand that times have changed. It is good to build churches, preach sermons, establish missions and schools, but all these labors **will be vain**, if we neglect **the most important** weapon of our time, i.e., the press." A cardinal of Pisa adds, "You preach a sermon on Sunday, as the newspapers preach one every day, every hour. You speak to the faithful in church, as the newspaper follows them in their homes. You speak for half an hour or an hour, as the newspaper never stops talking."

In our country, the matter of the Catholic press leaves very much to be desired. [...] We still lack **general agreement** in this work and mutual aid. On the part of society, there is still a great failure to comprehend the importance of this work, and the **sacrifice** proves **inadequate** for putting the Catholic press in Poland on strong footing. The Church's enemies have millions and billions (e.g., of dollars), whereas the worker in the domain of the Catholic press cannot exert his strength to perfect and enhance his work because he must simply fight for the material survival of his press activities. We have too few laypeople educated enough to work with a pen in the Catholic scene, and hence the output of the Catholic press in our country is still very, very modest. To prepare also lay workers and to ensure the publishers' material survival is perhaps the most burning matter in regard to the press.

Furthermore, the distribution is too weak. For they are few who would consider it their **duty** to extend the good press.

Finally, there is a great lack of genuinely Catholic public libraries, reading rooms, lending libraries, and bookstores. Indeed the heart aches when it sees downright scandalous books in window displays of the city lending libraries, and inside a long line of youth. And he who lends the books—is a Jew. This is another serious point in regard to the press, and it is all the more acute because it concerns the immediate poisoning of the hearts of youth.

May God grant that, in the near future, there will be no city or village that lacks libraries and reading rooms with an adequate supply of good books and periodicals, very cheap or free. Let circles arise everywhere having as their purpose to extend and promote the good press, and soon they would transform the face of the earth. Those to whom Almighty God has lent some fluency with the pen and ability in any field of literature, let them unite in an independent circle such that these gifts of God can be used to produce much good press in every field of writing. Of course one should not restrict oneself to the faithful, but should write also for non-Catholics and give them good spiritual nourishment. These are the current goals of the "Militia of the Immaculata," and by this means many conversions have already occurred.

25. Today's Enemies of the Church

[Autograph Manuscript, Kraków, before 22 X 1922]

In this brief paper I do not intend to talk about the internal enemies of the Church; I wish only to draw attention to the external enemies.

We are witnessing feverish actions directed against God's Church that, unfortunately, are not without fruit. They have innumerable apostles.

In the register of the Ministry of Religious Confessions and Public Education are recorded as many as fifteen of their groups: scholars of Sacred Scripture, Baptists, followers of the teaching of the first Christians, Adventists, Seventh-day Adventists, Johannites, Methodists, Church of God, Free Evangelical Church, Evangelical Christians, "*sztundyści karaimi*," "*duchoborcy*," Messianists, old ritualists (Old Believers, or "Old Catholics"), and the Church of Czech Brethren. They are not limited to preaching falsehood with the word, but also, and very abundantly, they are flooding our cities and villages with the most diverse publications in the form of magazines, brochures, leaflets, and even books. The various "America-Echo," "Watchtower," "New Way," "Gospel Thoughts," "Heralds of the Gospel," "Polish Reborn," etc., pass from hand to hand and poison the hearts of the faithful.

All this work, however, is only the preamble.

Behind these front lines goes the bulk of the enemy's army. Who is it? Perhaps at first glance it will seem exaggerated if I say that the prime, the greatest, and the most powerful enemy of the Church—is Freemasonry.

That the flood of Protestant sects is actually the vanguard of Freemasonry is explicitly admitted by the Masonic organization Free Thought. It says, "Reserving complete independence in our judgment of the intrinsic value of the teaching of the national church, we can, however, support its fight as well as every other Protestant sect against the supremacy of the Roman Church."

Who are the Freemasons?

The Popes have already given an assessment of them, the first on April 27, 1738: the Holy Father Clement XII in his bull *In Eminenti* accuses them of acting "under an imaginary appearance of natural honesty and under a strict and secret alliance." He also condemns Freemasonry and prohibits contact with the Masons under pain of excommunication ipso facto, reserved to the Pope.

And thirteen years later, Benedict XIV with his bull of March 18 *Providas Romanorum Pontificum* renews the condemnation issued by Clement XII, and the reasons given, among others, are that in Freemasonry "men of all religions and sects come together, and that, in the opinion of judicious and honest men, this sect is evil and corrupt."

Pope Pius VII issued two bulls, in 1813 (August 13) and in 1821 (September 13), in which he says the following: "It is not a secret to anyone what a multitude of malignant men have gathered together in these difficult times against the Lord and His Vicar, who especially aim, having seduced the faithful under the cover of philosophy, by vain deceitfulness, and having torn them away from the doctrine of the Church, to weaken and overthrow the same Church, although by futile endeavor. In order to achieve this more easily they have formed secret assemblies and covert sects, by which they were expecting to easily draw many into their societies of conspiracy and crime." And they strive to "give to each extensive freedom of judging by his own figment and fantasy the religion which he will profess, and having introduced indifference toward religion, of which there is nothing more fatal, they profane and desecrate the Passion of Jesus Christ with some iniquitous ceremonies, they despise the sacraments of the Church and the mysteries of the Catholic religion, and they overthrow this Holy Apostolic See, against which, as it has always wielded the primacy of the Apostolic Chair, they burn with some kind of odd hate and insidiously plot her destruction. Their moral principles are criminal. It promotes pleasures of lust, it permits killing anyone who has not kept the secret, it teaches that it is permitted, after raising a rebellion, to deprive of their power kings and all rulers, whom with great affront they commonly call tyrants."

However, this did not prevent them at all from wining over the rulers. Therefore, Pope Leo XII in his bull *Quo Graviora* of March 13, 1825, renewing the former papal condemnations, adds these words of warning to the rulers: "This is their sliest betrayal, that when they appear to be engaged with extending your power, then they are seeking most for the overturning of it. They try very much to convince the rulers to restrict and weaken the power of the other bishops and gradually appropriate the rights of the Pope and bishops. They do this not only from hatred toward the Pope but also so that the people subject to the ruling princes' scepter after the overthrow of ecclesiastical power are able to change and overturn the political form of government."

Likewise, Pius VIII with his bull *Traditi* (May 24, 1829), Gregory XVI with his bull *Mirari* (August 15, 1832), and Pius IX repeatedly (November 9, 1846; April 20, 1849; December 9, 1854; December 8, 1864; September 25, 1865; and November 21, 1873) have condemned Freemasonry.

Finally, Pope Leo XIII extensively discusses the issue of Freemasonry and condemns it with his bull *Humanum Genus* of April 20, 1884. In it the Pope asserts that "during a century and a half, Freemasonry became vastly large, and by using audacity and craftiness took control of all levels of social hierarchy and took in the bosom of the modern state a power almost equal to the monarch's."

And the Popes were not exaggerating!

Freemasonry was organized by British freethinkers in London in 1717, and only six years later in the General Constitutions it clearly had set itself a goal that nobody was allowed to change. "Each of the Grand Lodges," it states, "has the right to improve older regulations and establish new ones, but never to modify the fundamental points, which should remain forever and diligently be fulfilled." What are these fundamental points? They are the complete removal of the supernatural world. Obviously, then, there is no mention of religion or of morality.

At every step we see the trend toward this goal. Art, literature, periodicals, theaters, cinemas, youth education, and legislation are rapidly heading toward the elimination of the supernatural world and the indulgence of the flesh.

No wonder, because Freemasonry has branched out extensively. [...]

* * *

In Poland, in 1810 there were already twelve known lodges. [...]

Ministers, generals, and other dignitaries, such as the military and civilian in the nation, appear on the list of members. [...]

All of these belong indeed to Freemasonry and cause much harm, but they are not part of its real head. These are the so-called blue Masons, while the so-called red masonry is restricted to a small number of people, mostly Jews, who, fully aware of their goals, direct the entire large host of those more or less "enlightened" in regard to the Masonic organization. The head is unknown and always acts secretly in order to make opposition impossible. They make the plans of action. From their workshop emerged the French Revolution, the series of revolutions from 1789 to 1815..., and also the World War. Voltaire, D'Alembert, Rousseau, Diderot, Choiseul, Pombal, Aralda, Tanucci, Hangwitz, Byron, Mazzini, Palmerston, Garibaldi, and others worked according to their indications. [...]

Freemasonry exalts the people they favor and throws them down when they desire to act on their own. Napoleon himself personally experienced this very acutely.

How can we counteract this plague, this army of the Antichrist?

The Immaculata, Mediatrix of all graces, can and wants to help. For what purpose were the apparition in Lourdes and the apparition of the Miraculous Medal, through which so many have already been converted? A soul, conquered by love for Her, certainly will resist moral corruption, the principal Masonic weapon. "We will not conquer the Church by reasoning," they decided in one of their conventions, "but by the corruption of morals."

Also worthy of reflection are the predictions of [Ven.] Wanda Malczewska, recorded by Fr. Gregory Augustynik, who personally knew her, and which in part have indeed been fulfilled. In them Our Lord Jesus recommends, "Let associations of women be formed—and separately of men—for different states, but with one spirit, under the protection of my Mother, immaculately conceived, in order to eradicate lechery and promote the virtue of chastity and defend it. Whoever loves God and country, I beseech him, by my cruel scourging and crowning with thorns, let him become a member of this association—let him guard for himself the virtue of chastity and extirpate licentiousness, and encourage others to do this."

And Fr. Urban in the December issue dedicated to the Immaculate Conception is convinced that the only salvation from the dominion of Satan that is spreading in today's world is ardent veneration and imitation of the Immaculata.

26. The Archconfraternity of the Holy Rosary

[Autograph Manuscript, Grodno, 1922–1925]

The Eastern borderlands, where we currently reside, detest the Rosary, and they are steeped in the schism. The Archconfraternity of the Holy Rosary is needed here all the more, to expand the mission of prayer and spread as widely as possible this sublime way of praying. Maybe also the schismatics, understanding it more closely, will begin to think about it differently. In this conference, therefore, I will briefly offer a few words about the Rosary and Archconfraternity of the Rosary.

Originally the Rosary was called Mary's psalter, because as David's psalter is composed of 150 psalms, so also in the Rosary we find 150 Hail Marys. According to legend, the following incident contributed to the name change: A pious young man had a habit of frequently adorning an image of the Blessed Virgin Mary with roses. He later joined a monastery. Within the walls of the monastery, he no longer had the opportunity to bring flowers to Mary; this grieved him very much. While he was afflicted in this way, the Blessed Virgin Mary appeared to him and said, "Recite devoutly my psalter, and adorn me with the most beautiful flowers." He began therefore to recite the Rosary, and immediately he saw how for each Hail Mary the Blessed Virgin Mary took from his mouth a rose of wondrous beauty and weaved with those roses a garland for Herself. At the Our Father She wove into the garland a resplendent lily. This was the origin of the <u>name</u> "Rosary."

In addition to the Lord's Prayer and the Angelic Salutation, the <u>essence</u> of the Rosary is contemplating the mysteries of the life of Christ Our Lord and the Most Holy Mother of God. The document of the erection of the archconfraternity clearly speaks about this when it defines the Rosary as (*orandi unam quo*) "*Sanctissima Virgo Maria Mater Dei centum quinquaginta salutationibus angelicis, praemissa singulis denis oratione dominica additisque piis mysteriorum*

Iesu Christi Salvatoris nostri, eiusdem sanctissimae Matris meditationibus honoratur" [(a prayer in which) "the Most Holy Virgin Mary, Mother of God, is honored by a hundred and fifty Angelic Salutations, each decade preceded by the Lord's Prayer and combined with devout meditation on the mysteries of Jesus Christ our Savior, and of His Most Holy Mother"]. The Sacred Congregation of Indulgences [1] points out that meditation on the mysteries is indispensable for gaining the indulgences. To facilitate this meditation, in the sixteenth century the holy Spaniard Martin Navarrus (1491–1586) added to each Hail Mary after the name "Jesus" a very brief mention of the mystery at hand—e.g., "thou, Virgin, conceived by the Holy Spirit," "thou, Virgin, who went to Elizabeth."

The <u>origin</u> of the Rosary is well known. A contemporary witness, Fr. Tiery of Alpola, a Dominican, recounts it. He says that St. Dominic could not in a particular locality convert the heretics; he turned to the Blessed Virgin Mary, whom he had highly revered since his childhood, and asked for assistance. The Queen of Heaven then appeared to him, showed him the rosary, and instructed him to propagate it. He fervently set to work, and from that time he recovered with ease a great many souls who had strayed, so that soon their number exceeded one hundred thousand. The whole Catholic world eagerly received the Holy Rosary, and innumerable graces and miracles of conversion testified to its supernatural origin.

<u>The Popes have highly recommended it</u>, and as Hadrian VI asserts, "the Rosary defeats Satan." Paul III said, "Through the Rosary of St. Dominic, God's wrath toward France and Italy was restrained," and Julius III proclaims, "The Rosary is the ornament of the Roman Church." Gregory XIV: "The Rosary is the eradication of sin, the recovery of grace, the increase of God's glory." Paul V: "The Rosary is a treasure of graces." Urban VIII: "Through the Rosary, the number of most fervent Christians increases." Pius IX: "If you desire peace to reign in your hearts and families, gather together each evening to recite the Rosary." Pope Leo XIII in his encyclical on the Rosary says, "We strongly urge all the faithful, whether it be publicly in the churches or in private homes and within the family,

to pray the Rosary, and as far as possible to not relent in this holy exercise."

[...] Religious associations are multiplying from day to day, and this is one of the proofs of the vitality of Holy Church, but sometimes they may lack adequate coordination and harmonious cooperation. Consequently, in our times, when the Church's enemies join forces and work together, we ought to pay deeper attention to the words of the Holy Father Benedict XV in his encyclical issued on the occasion of the 700th anniversary of the founding of the Third Order: "Why should...as well...the very numerous and varied associations existing worldwide under the name Catholic, either of youth or of workers or of women, not unite with the Third Order, to thus more intensely work for the glory of Jesus Christ and the welfare of the Church, with the same zeal whereby Francis was imbued with the desire for peace and charity?" It is not here about merging into one mass but rather creating one strong, although organically differentiated, body. If we arrived at this, Catholic associations would become a great power.

[1] July 22, 1908, ASS 41-676.

27. THE ROSARY

[Manuscript, Niepokalanów, 8 VIII 1933]

[...] The Rosary, therefore, is an easy prayer, because it is not difficult to repeat the above-mentioned prayers; however, it is also a very sublime prayer, because by its recitation one contemplates the mysteries of the Faith. He who is more intelligent and more familiar in matters of the Faith can more deeply contemplate these mysteries and possibly discover in them a greater number of practical suggestions for his life.

Can a pagan pray the Rosary? Why not. Indeed, in that case he more easily and deeply learns about the truths of the Faith, and by praying he obtains more easily the grace to know the truth in religious matters and the strength to accept this religion, which he will come to know as true, regardless of the difficulties and opinions of others who do not yet understand matters of the Faith.

In October, Catholics have the custom of venerating the Most Holy Mother by reciting the Rosary in churches or in private homes, and even the Immaculata, manifesting Herself at Lourdes in 1858, appeared with rosary in hand, thus encouraging us by Her own example to recite it. We therefore surely give great pleasure to the Mother of God and draw down upon ourselves and our families many blessings from God when we recite the Rosary.

Korube

28. MI

[Autograph Manuscript, Mugenzai no Sono, circa 12 VI, 1934]

Maria

MI in general, MI 1, MI 2, MI 3.

MI in general, according to the diploma. Consecrate oneself to the Immaculata as an instrument; be Hers.

MI 1: Without commitments, according to one's lesser or greater zeal—individual action—without heroism—with limitations. Union with Her will, fulfillment of Her will, according to the degree of zeal.

MI 2: Commitments according to a statute of the association—collective action—without heroism, with limitations. Union, fulfillment of Her will also according to a statute of the association.

MI 3: <u>Unlimitedness</u> of the gift of oneself—therefore also heroic action and unlimited perfection—become Her ever more perfectly—become Her, as She is of God and perfectly united to God (in a Catholic sense-divinization in Her and through Her). Union, unlimited fulfillment of Her will. The perfect MI. A force without limits.

Omnia possum in Eo, qui me per Immaculatam confortat [I can do all things in Him, who strengthens me through the Immaculata]. *(Principium omnis boni Deus Pater per Filium, per Spiritum Sanctum), (per Iesum per Immaculatam)...* [(The principle of every good is God the Father through the Son, through the Holy Ghost), (through Jesus, through the Immaculata)...]

MI through the Immaculata—recognizes Her perfection, perfect immaculateness—God's will and Her will *convertuntur* [are interchangeable]—recognizes God's perfection, in creating Her so perfect, immaculate, without the slightest stain. A great pleasure and glory for the Most Holy Spirit as Her spouse. The Most Holy Trinity's great glory. Hence also an abundance of graces. In practice, the expression: the Immaculata's will, fulfill Her will, rely upon Her will, as She wishes, etc. The recognition of the universal mediation of all graces.

Love the Immaculata for the love of the Most Sacred Heart of Our Lord Jesus, in order to render Him the most pleasure, to fulfill His will, to follow the path that He has indicated by His example and teaching, to obtain the strength to carry out His commands.

29. [DIRECTIVE FOR THE *SMALL DAILY*]

[Autograph Manuscript, Niepokalanów, 1936]

Maria

To fight evil in the spirit of the MI, of the Immaculata, with love toward everyone, even the worst. To emphasize and more greatly praise the good, so that our example attracts others to God, rather than spreads the evil. When it comes, however, to drawing the attention of our society or the authorities to a given evil, do this delicately and with love toward the person who did the evil. Do not exaggerate, and do not go further into the details of the evil than what is needed for its remedy.

Articles

First issue of Polish *Rycerz Niepokalanej* (Knight of the Immaculata), January 1922

First issue of Japanese *Knight, Seibo no Kishi*, May 24, 1930

30. From the Editor

[Rycerz Niepokalanej, January 1922, p. 3]

[...] The purpose of *Knight of the Immaculata* is not only to deepen and strengthen our faith, to indicate the true form of asceticism, and to familiarize the faithful with Christian mysticism, but also, in accordance with the principles of the "Militia of the Immaculata," it is to strive for the conversion of anti-Catholics. The tone of the magazine will always be friendly toward everyone regardless of differences of religious belief or nationality. The love that Christ taught is its distinctive feature. And it is for the sake of this love for the wayward that, desiring happiness for souls, it will seek to stigmatize lies, to illuminate the truth, and to show the true way to happiness.

[...] Gracious benefactors: the Immaculata and the souls that this magazine will lead to truth and happiness on this earth and forever in heaven will repay you generously.

31. Where Is Happiness?

[Rycerz Niepokalanej, January 1922, pp. 4–5]

Everyone desires happiness and aspires to it, but few find it, because they do not seek it where it is.

Let us go to the street. On a wide sidewalk are people of various ages and conditions in great haste, and each of them aims at some purpose, which should be a particle of his happiness. In the middle of the street are moving carriages and cars, and those who sit in them dream of—happiness. In the display windows are offered all kinds of goods to the passersby in order to bring the sellers and buyers—happiness. Wherever you look, you see people thirsting for—

happiness. But are all these sure that at the end of their diversions they will embrace the so-very-desirable treasure?

One of these people has set for himself an objective for the accumulation of material goods—money. He has not yet reached the end of his desires—so he continues to pursue it. But will he ever reach it?... The more goods he accumulates, the more he impresses himself with them, the more he desires. And even if he possessed the whole world, he would still look enviously at the moon. He desires more and more—to acquire them ever more quickly and to possess them ever longer. How much labor, worry, sacrifice, health it has cost him to possess what he has, and how much toil still awaits him! And what if sickness visits him, fortune turns its back on him, a thief robs him? Eventually—in the end, death also will come. And then?... He will have to leave everything and go by himself into eternity... The very thought of it poisons his brief moments of pleasure derived from the advantages gained. He does not possess, therefore, happiness!

Let us move on. On a door is a poster: "Dance Party," and many gather there. Enjoy the world, while you can! But are they happy? Do they not desire a greater, fuller, and sweeter cup of delights? They are searching for ever newer pleasures, yet eventually they fall into a glut, they feel—the limit. And yet they would like happiness without limits and without end...

And therefore, they do not find it.

Perhaps worldly glory will satisfy man? Let us take a glance at the ranks of respectable people, occupying lofty positions and enjoying much popularity. Perhaps they possess the talisman of happiness? Let us ask them whether or not they would wish their glory to embrace wider horizons, to shine forth in other fields? Undoubtedly every one of them would willingly accept this opportunity, and perhaps at times consider how to make it shine still more. Meanwhile, perhaps others cast a shadow on them; many do not appreciate their achievements; so many less deserving individuals are placed above them...finally—human glory also is a crystal that is very fragile: many who had formerly been famous now find themselves in the shadow of oblivion. And in the end they too will be visited by—death... And after it?... Of what benefit will be human praise and monuments, if your eternity is unhappy?

And in this, therefore, there is no happiness.

Moreover, wealth, the pleasures of life, and worldly glory are the exceptions in life rather than the shared lot, though everyone desires happiness...

※ ※ ※

Man's heart is too great to be filled by money, sensuality, or the smoke of worldly glory, which is deceitful though mesmerizing. The heart desires a higher good, one without limits and which lasts forever. And this good is only—God.

Fr. M. K.

32. Greatness and Sanctity

[Rycerz Niepokalanej, April 1922, pp. 66–68]

Every saint is a great man, but not every great man was also a saint, even though he might have greatly served mankind. But there are many similarities between them. I am not speaking of well-known people who accumulated many possessions or were known for their physical strength or are remembered by mankind as great achievers, but were—malefactors or downright criminal, although sometimes they are driven by criminal ingenuity in order to—become famous. I will consider only the geniuses of human thought.

The genius and the saint have much in common. They rise above their surroundings, they naturally attract the attention of others—they are special and truly extraordinary people. Both have uncommon drive to reach their goals and an abundance of trust in the rich gifts of nature and grace. They strive to achieve their goals through thorns and all kinds of obstacles and difficulties. Not only people jealous by nature but sometimes even their best friends in good faith hinder or slow them down on their march. Both, if they climb to the top and reach the desired peak or draw near to their goal, will see followers who look up to them and will follow in their footsteps. And the memory of a saint and a genius passes from generation to generation. History tells us about such people who were both saint and genius, such as St. Paul, St. Augustine, St. Thomas, St. Gregory the Great, and many others.

But there is a fundamental difference between the saint and the genius who does not strive for holiness. The genius's dream—is fame. For him, it is toward the approval of men that he exerts his mind, devotes his time, applies his abilities, and sometimes endures very heavy sacrifices. Perfecting himself in one way, he often neglects the most important aspects, and he thus destroys the balance and harmony in himself, and at times even causes damage to those of others through his disorder. A saint, on the contrary, always has God's glory in mind. He pays no heed to the opinions of men and places himself above these. He correctly subordinates the faculties of the soul and body and the body itself to reason, and this reason he subjects to God's governance. Hence, he gains for himself peace.

When the storm breaks out and the thunder of disrespect, of anger and hateful envy, comes from all sides, when slander and contempt strike and friends turn away, or even unite themselves with your enemies against you, then a genius bends under his burden, grieves bitterly, suffers and feels unhappy. A saint stands above all this. He also at times experiences pain, but soon consoles himself in prayer and, trusting in God, peacefully strides onward.

A more serious illness visits, old age crushes—the genius often ceases to be a genius; his intellectual faculties wane. A saint always moves forward without regard to the state of his health or his age. Indeed, illnesses and afflictions are for him a ladder to greater perfection; in their fire he is purified like gold.

The heritage of the genius brings profit to mankind, but very often harm as well. Napoleon was a commander-genius, but how many tears he evoked, how much blood he shed, and in the end, he left his homeland weakened. In our times, railroads, printing presses, telegraphs, telephones, etc., instead of disseminating education, have become the sowers of falsehood and moral decay. How many not-to-be-forgotten literary talents have aided in destroying order and turning their readers away from their Creator? How many souls of youth have been poisoned by their books and magazines?... A saint always spends his time "doing good," after the example of Jesus; wherever he goes, he plants seeds of truth and happiness and draws souls, with his own example, toward Uncreated Goodness.

Not everyone can become a genius, but the way to sanctity is open to all.

These are the common and differing points between a genius and a saint; to erase these differences in people of our nation with great talent—is to prepare [them to reach] the summit of man's greatness: a genius-saint.

M. K.

33. Goal of the MI

[Rycerz Niepokalanej, April 1922, pp. 78–79]

It is good and necessary, the right thing, to think also about the missions in Asia and Africa; but we mustn't forget about those who live among us who, like the pagans, need help. Many of them do not know the true Church of Christ, and therefore fight against it. To offer a loving hand to these unfortunate ones—here is the goal of the "Militia of the Immaculata."

When all schismatics and Protestants profess the Catholic Faith with deep conviction, when all Jews living among us will voluntarily ask for holy baptism—a part of the goal of the "Militia of the Immaculata" will be attained.

34. The First Condition

[Rycerz Niepokalanej, May 1922, pp. 102–103]

The MI's goal is so difficult to achieve that if one were to rely only on natural strength, activity, and endeavors, the possibility of arriving at it would seem doubtful. Daily experience teaches us, in fact, that the Church's enemies have more natural means and, according to Christ's words, are often wiser than the children of light. Further, for conversion and sanctification, grace is necessary, but our corrupt nature itself is inclined to sin. Therefore, one can rely only on help from above. And the easiest and surest source of help in this matter is, by God's will, the Blessed Virgin Mary. To Her Holy Church applies the words of Sacred Scripture, "She shall crush thy head" (i.e., of the infernal serpent), and of Her the Church sings, "Thou alone hast destroyed all heresies throughout the world." "All," thus without exception; "heresies," thus not heretics, for these She loves; "alone," thus She will be sufficient; "destroyed," thus not merely weakened, and that throughout the entire world. The head of all the varied members of the infernal dragon is undoubtedly in our times—Freemasonry. And She shall crush this head. Further, history teaches us that there was hardly a conversion in which Mary's hand was not particularly seen. All the saints fostered a special devotion to Her, and the Holy Father Leo XIII says in an encyclical on the Rosary (September 22, 1891), "It can be affirmed that from the immense treasure of all grace...nothing is given to us by the will of God, except through Mary, and as no one can approach the Most High Father but by the Son, so ordinarily no one can approach Christ but by His Mother." Can we, therefore, pursue the MI's goal in any way other than giving ourselves to the Blessed Virgin Mary Immaculate—unconditionally, totally, and forever as an instrument in Her immaculate hands, so that in us and through us, She alone may deign to act? Therefore, this consecration constitutes the MI's essence.

35. God's Grace and the Saints' Natural Gifts

[Rycerz Niepokalanej, June 1922, pp. 114–117]

To every man on this earth, God has entrusted a specific mission—when He created the universe, He so directed the first causes that an uninterrupted chain of effects would create the most appropriate conditions and circumstances for this mission's fulfillment. Therefore, every man is born with abilities suited to and in keeping with his task, and so throughout his whole life the environment and circumstances—everything—arrange themselves so as to make it possible and easy for him to attain his goal. And it is precisely in the attainment of this goal that all human perfection is to be found; the more thoroughly he accomplishes his task and the more perfectly he fulfills his mission, the greater and holier he is in God's eyes.

Besides the natural gifts, man is also accompanied from the cradle to the tomb by God's grace, which is poured out upon each one of us in such quantity and quality that our frail human capacities may strengthen themselves and acquire the supernatural vigor necessary to confront our own mission.

And many saints throughout their lives have always cooperated with God's gifts, whether natural or supernatural. Here I am not thinking only of the Most Pure Mother of God, who by a special privilege was Immaculate from the time of Her conception—not even the slightest sin defiled Her soul. I am thinking also of the hosts of pure souls, such as St. Aloysius and our fellow countryman St. Stanislaus Kostka—they stood before God's court in the robe of innocence received in holy baptism.

However, among the saints, there are those who for a longer or shorter period of time abused God's gifts and were deaf to the inner call of grace. Some of them were too attached to their occupations or amusements, even if not sinful, and were forgetful of their sublime destiny—such as the seraphic St. Francis, the favorite among the rich youth of Assisi. Others, falling low and wallowing in the mud of vice, totally distanced themselves from God, like St. Mary Magdalene and St. Margaret of Cortona. Finally, others did not even know the true way chosen for them, like St. Paul the Apostle, who openly confessed that it was because of ignorance that he persecuted God's Church.

And let us now see how God pursued them with His grace, how, in favorable circumstances, He knocked upon the doors of their hearts, more clearly showing them their mission—and when they began to cooperate with the gifts of God, they became saints. And so St. Francis hears a voice calling him to combat, and when he obeys and prepares his horse and armor—God explains to him that he will have to lead a spiritual army and fight with it against the powers of hell: and here begins another life. St. Margaret of Cortona sees the stinking corpse of her lover and, moved by the sight, abandons her sinful life and—converts. And when St. Paul in the greatest ferocity is approaching the gates of Damascus to imprison the Christians there and then is struck to the ground, he who was once a bitter enemy becomes the zealous apostle of Christ's teaching. And all these saints after their conversion no longer measured and placed limits on their service to Almighty God: their former mediocre righteousness did not satisfy them. By climbing to the noblest heights of Christian perfection, they tried to make up for the time and the graces previously squandered. For God's glory and the salvation of souls, no effort is too heavy for them, no cross is unpleasant—from now on everything is a pleasure to them, everything is a treasure, because everything is in the service of God's love!

The roads by which God leads His saints to their sublime destiny are various and countless. Often He strengthens our natural inclinations with supernatural gifts and allows and commands us to use them—but sometimes of these natural inclinations He asks sacrifice, if this is necessary for a higher development of our soul. "Almighty God," says Bossuet, "if He wishes to make people worthy of Himself, must mold them variously, so that they are formed according to His plan; in the midst of this task He has only one consideration: He does not directly inflict violence on our innate dispositions." Hence, God led some out to the desert and completely secluded them from other people, and some He called to a common life and mutual assistance in their progress toward perfection. Others He has left in the whirl of the world, at the plow, in workshops, or at royal tables. Some He made famous for their secular or religious science, or for their social activity, and others He left in the shadow of oblivion throughout their lives. Some He caressed, so to speak, nourishing them with the milk of spiritual consolations, and others He fed with the hard bread of suffering. All depends on the needs of the individual soul and on the type of mission for which it has been destined.

The saints, even though they faithfully followed the inspiration of divine grace, do not cease to be people similar to us, and usually their deeds and words carry the characteristics of their environment, their country, their homeland. For example, St. Catherine of Siena, having in herself the "Sienese blood"—which according to the expression of St. Bernard is "sweet blood"—sometimes lavished children with her kisses, and when one day she was called to comfort a person sentenced to death and to persuade him to go to confession, all night long, as a dearest mother with her child, she held his head to her chest. In St. Teresa, as another example, what stands out is chivalry. Coming from "Avila, the city of knights," where even the women in the absence of their husbands were able to withstand a siege, she thoroughly acquired the spirit of her own city and country; hence, we often find in her writings the expressions "God of battles," "the banner of God," "to serve God with manly courage." The same can be seen in St. Ignatius Loyola, a former soldier and a fellow countryman of St. Teresa.

Many saints were lovers of music. Sometimes when St. Francis was inspired, he took in his hands two pieces of wood and played them like a violin. St. Teresa on holidays played a small flute and a drum, and St. Ignatius Loyola was so carried away by music that he no longer felt any suffering.

Usually the saints of God acted quite naturally; however, for the love of a higher virtue, and especially to escape from human praise and recognition, under the influence of grace they have taken upon themselves actions that, in the opinion of the world, are irrational and degrading. A veritable master in this regard was St. Philip Neri. For example, when Polish delegates sent to the Pope had learned about the "saint" who was residing in Rome, they wanted to see him. St. Philip, warned about this, prepared a seat for himself with books, and, surrounded by children, he instructed one of the boys to read him a book of jokes, while he attentively listened. The delegates entered with reverence, but the saint did not allow the boy to stop reading, and he asked the guests to wait. However, when chapter followed chapter and it was not possible for the delegates to wait any longer, they departed, upset and bewildered. The saint thanked Almighty God that he had eluded human praise.

So we see how the saints walked in different paths, how they dealt with their natural gifts in different ways. There was one thing they all had in common, though: they always subordinated their natural gifts to grace—that grace which often lifted them out of many years of laziness or even slavery to sin. Therefore, they all lived a superior and supernatural life, regardless of whether their path was compatible with their nature—grace had required them to walk it: their only purpose was God and His holy love. Everything else—their natural and supernatural doings, pleasant or unpleasant—were to help them reach their goal. And yes, nothing could harm them; on the contrary, the advantages were infinite, because they were spiritual, and they found these advantages in everything, because "to them that love God, everything cooperates unto good, to those who according to purpose are called to be saints" (Rom 8:28).

M. K.

36. The First Nativity Play and the First Shepherd's Mass

[Rycerz Niepokalanej, December 1922, pp. 233–234]

When the evening of Christmas Eve comes upon the cities and villages, and the first star glitters in the sky, in almost every Polish home near the Christmas tree a crèche is seen. From house to house goes a group of boys in costume—performing the nativity play or carrying around a small crèche and singing Christmas carols. At midnight, crowds everywhere set out in the dim moonlight for the church, the frozen snow crunching underfoot—they are going to the Shepherd's Mass. And in the church by the manger Holy Mass is celebrated.

From where do these traditions come?

The crèche and the Shepherd's Mass date back to the thirteenth century; they began with St. Francis of Assisi.

Christmas day was for him always a day of special joy. "If I knew the emperor," he would often say, "I would ask him to issue the order that on this day grain be scattered for all the birds, especially the swallows, and that anyone who has cattle in the barn must, in memory of Christ's birth in a stable, give from his possessions nourishment more abundant than usual. I would like also that all the rich of this world receive the poor at their table on that solemn day!" [1]

In Greccio, John Velita, a friend of the saint, had offered him a wooded hill as a place to live. While there, St. Francis, during the Christmas festival of 1223, called for this man and said to him, "Look, I would like to celebrate with you the Christmas festival, and I have arrived at the following idea: in the forest near our hermitage you will find a cave; there you will place a manger filled with hay, and there you must also bring an ox and a donkey, just as in Bethlehem. If I could once see with my own eyes how the divine Child lay in the manger—the Lord condemned to misery and poverty for love of us!"

Willingly, John Velita complied with this request, and the holy father Francis, having received the prior permission of the Apostolic See, built with the help of the brothers an altar and invited the people of the surrounding area. At midnight, great crowds of people came with torches in hand, and the brothers with lighted candles surrounded the grotto. Holy Mass commenced. "When a passage from the Gospel was being sung, an eyewitness, Thomas of Celano [2], tells that Francis appeared in the vestments of a deacon. Sighing deeply, permeated with the ardor of devotion and beaming with interior joy, the saint stood before the manger, and his voice rose above the crowds, teaching them about where they must look for the highest good. He spoke with the ineffable sweetness of the Infant Jesus, of the Great King who deigned to take upon Himself our human nature, of the Christ from the city of David. And whenever he was to pronounce the name of Jesus, an interior ardor of his heart brought to his lips the words 'Child of Bethlehem'; this expression on his lips took on a strange charm. He stood before the people, like the Lamb of God, in the full holiness of His sacrifice. At the end of the celebration all returned with hearts filled with heavenly joy."

This was the first Shepherd's Mass by the first "crib of Bethlehem." The sons of St. Francis, imitating their seraphic father, spread throughout the world this lovely method of honoring the Infant Jesus.

M. K.

[1] Celano, "Vita Secunda" II, 151; Speculum Perfectionis, 124.
[2] "Vita Prima" LXXX.

37. Threatening Danger

[Rycerz Niepokalanej, January 1923, pp. 2–4]

Considering recent events, it is clear that things are going wrong in our country: prices increase daily, the country leans toward economic collapse, the government is weak and incompetent—we feel that a mysterious hand always collides with us and draws us to ruin.

All over the globe—here more weakly, there more fiercely—a battle against the Church and the happiness of souls goes on. The enemy manifests himself in various guises and under different names. It is generally known how socialism takes advantage of the miserable condition of the worker in order to infect him with the poison of disbelief. We see how the Bolsheviks trample on religion. We hear the teachings of the materialists, who wish to reduce the universe to only that which we know immediately through the senses and thus persuade themselves and others that there is no God and that man has no soul. Theosophy instills religious indifference, and the Sacred Scripture scholars and other Protestants with loads of money are winning over to themselves followers. All these camps form a compact battle line against the Church.

[...] When we are faced with such powerful attacks of the enemies of God's Church, are we allowed to stand around idle? Is it permissible to merely whine and shed tears? No, let us remember that at the divine judgment, not only will we give a strict account of the activities performed, but also Almighty God will count all the good deeds that we could have done but—<u>neglected</u>. Upon each of us rests the holy <u>obligation</u> to stand on the ramparts and with our own breast offer defense against the attempts of the enemy.

Sometimes one hears the question, "What can I do?" Such a strong organization, they have so much capital, etc. He who asks this question has perhaps forgotten what St. Paul said: "I can do all things in Him, who strengthens me."

How should we, especially members of the Militia of the Immaculata, fight? Perhaps, rendering an eye for an eye, go forth with the force of our fists? No, this is not our task. The purpose that the Knighthood of the Immaculata has set for itself is to conquer hearts for Her; She will do the rest. As for those unfortunate ones who in their stupidity and anger lift their hand against the best Father, to satisfy their cravings and gain some little bit of happiness, let them only do or endure anything, even the smallest thing, for Her—a breach is already made, She has now a right to take, sweetly and over time, possession of that heart, and She will place it in the burning Heart of Jesus and make it happy. Out of love toward the bad we will <u>with all our energy</u>, insofar as possible, oppose all their evil actions; we will commend these hearts to the Immaculata with prayer and suffering, <u>not counting the cost</u>, conquering for Her their soul—and they, already here on earth, will be infinitely grateful to us. More than once I have experienced this, and anyone who will bring such happiness to a person's soul will see how grateful this person will be.

Still, be careful not to suffer, work, and endure sacrifices for this appreciation. It would be too low an incentive. For God only, for God through the Immaculata and as an instrument in Her hand, live, suffer, work, and die—this is an ideal worthy of a Knight of the Immaculata.

Rycerz Niepokalanej

38. Does God Exist?

[Rycerz Niepokalanej, January 1923, pp. 5–7]

(While I was traveling for some days, I frequently spoke about the truths of the Faith with unbelievers and Catholics; so now the "Knight" will resume in its columns at least some of these conversations. I won't hold myself in these to a chronological order, but rather by a logical connection I will bring them together. In turn, for those who took part in them, I ask that they please give me their account, if I did not sufficiently re-create the thread of the argument.)

We had passed through Przemysl, and the train was rapidly carrying us toward Kraków. Near the window were sitting on either side two young men. One of them was an artist—a painter, a portraitist—and as we found out from the conversation, a Jew. We discussed man's purpose and came to the conclusion that it is to become similar to God, that is, God's external glory is actually this goal and is the creature's only complete happiness. At one station an intelligent man came into our compartment and sat down opposite me; he immediately joined our circle.

—But can we know whether Almighty God exists? - he asked.

—Of course.

—Someone can perhaps only believe in this; in fact, nobody can prove that Almighty God exists.

—If you please, sir, I will clearly prove it to you.

—In this regard, no one will convince me.

—Probably, sir, you refuse in advance all arguments.

—Not at all.

—I also would like to hear a clear proof of this - a lady sitting beside us interjected.

—Excuse me, gentlemen - I said, turning to those seated by the window - later, I will go back to the question that we were discussing, so that presently I can satisfy the desire of those who have just boarded.

—We would be very pleased.

—Firstly, however, excuse my asking, but what education do you have?

—I studied law at the university.

—And maybe philosophy also?

—No, not philosophy; but what does philosophy have to do with faith?

—Faith must be in harmony with reason and precisely for this philosophy is useful, especially on the question of whether Almighty God exists. But now I must know what we all agree on, for I must start from there; otherwise, we would be building on a precarious foundation.

So we begin:

—Do you exist, sir?

—Yes, but I am only a part of the earth.

—Please, sir, we will speak later about what we are; for now, I am only asking whether you exist.

—Yes, I do.

—And you, ma'am?

—I also affirm this.

—And perhaps one of you thinks otherwise?

Everyone nods in agreement.

—So our existence is certain.

—I would not say that.

—And why not?

—Because, in general, we cannot know anything with certainty; what one claims, others deny.

—Then you are not sure that you exist?

—I'm only a small particle of the matter in the universe.

—It does not concern me here - I repeat - what you are, but in general whether you exist, i.e., whether you are something or nothing.

—Obviously, I'm not nothing.

—For certain?

—For certain.

—And do you have a watch?

—I do - he answers, reaching into his pocket.

—Is it yours?
—It is mine.
—And for certain?
—Without a doubt.
—Pardon me, but if you had a doubt about it, I would ask you for it and put it in my pocket - (those present laugh). - Therefore, your premise that we cannot know anything for certain is false, for you consider your own existence to be an axiom and have no desire at all to doubt that this watch belongs to you. And I, do I exist?
—...Yes.
—And this lady, that gentleman, and in general all of us here present?
—They too.
—And for certain?
—...For certain.
—Why do you say that?
—Because...my eyes clearly tell me.
—And these fields, and meadows, passing by in the windows of our carriage, and the whole world and the stars above our heads: do they exist?
—They too; in general, I must admit now that what we see must exist; however, Almighty God we do not see.
—Pardon me, sir, but is the locomotive at the head of this train running?
—Obviously it is.
—For certain?
—For certain.
—Yet do you see it?
—No, but if it were not, our carriage would not be moving forward.
—Therefore, sir, you admit now that not only can we know something by directly seeing it, but also that reason can arrive at the knowledge of a given cause from its effect: correct?
—Yes, that's so.

—Sir, what would you think of a man who thought about his watch like this: "This metal cover by mere chance came out of the mine; it melted by itself in a strange coincidence and purified and shaped itself according to its present form. Also, the inscription was engraved on it by chance. The glass also was melted down and ground by chance. Also, the gears were made by themselves. And the other components of the watch were formed by the purest chance and then assembled into this well-ordered device, and so without need of a human mind or hand, all by chance, it indicates the hour." If this man were to claim this in all earnest, what would you say about him?

—That perhaps he suffers from a mental disturbance.

—Well, in nature we have organisms that are formed with vastly more intricacy. Certainly you marveled, in studying anatomy, the structure of even the human eye. How many different parts there are, how delicate they are, and how magnificently they provide our vision. All of nature is composed of millions and billions of organisms that live, develop, and reproduce. Could one affirm, therefore, that these marvels of nature are an accident? One could say, "All this does not happen without a cause": that is true, but these causes have still their own causes, and these also have their causes. But still in this series of causes, even if taken to infinity, must we not acknowledge a First Cause? The causes, in fact, by themselves do not give any perfection, but only give what they have themselves received, and what interests us is the author of that perfection. A First Cause must exist...and...it is God.

—This is obvious.

On the face of this gentleman, one could see a sort of wonder that hitherto he had not come to such a conclusion; perhaps he would have never thought of this truth.

M. K.

39. The Church and Socialism

[Rycerz Niepokalanej, February 1923, pp. 17–21]

Sometimes you hear the question, "Why does the Church condemn socialism?" And this question was put to me not too long ago. I promised to give an answer in the *Knight*, so let us now abide by the promise.

The nature of short articles does not allow me to extensively discuss the beginnings, the essence, the development, and the various phenomena of socialism, so I will limit myself to a summary presentation of its fundamental principles in their relationship to the Church. Every system, whether political or economic, or ultimately social, must be based on the essential real state of things, and not paying homage to unfounded assertions and dreams of exuberant imaginations. And yet socialism is lacking precisely in this.

Unsubstantiated assertions—it is repeated endlessly and never demonstrated that there is no God, no immortal soul, no life beyond the grave, no heaven, no hell, etc. These, according to Mussolini, are now obsolete for our time, yet they continue to linger in the minds of the masses; and on these principles rises socialism. Let us listen to the masters. Bebel: "It is not the gods who have created man, but man who has created the gods and God" (*Die Frau* 426). Liebknecht: "As for me, I got rid of religion a long time ago. I come from a time when German students were initiated early in the principles of atheism" (*Volksblatt* 1890 #281). Hoffmann considers the mystery of the Holy Trinity, the divinity of Jesus, the immortality of the soul, and eternal salvation as the most utopian of the utopias. Dietzgen: "If religion is based on faith in extraterrestrial, celestial beings and higher forces, spirits and gods, then democracy must be without religion." And a friend of Marx, *Leon Frankel*, writes in his own manifesto, "I believe neither in heaven nor in hell, neither in reward nor in punishment" (*Vorwärts* 1896 p. 81). And at a parliamentary meeting on December 31, 1881, Bebel clearly said, "In the political field we strive for a republic, in the economic field for socialism, and in what is called the religious sphere, for atheism."

So the socialist's field of vision, in accordance with his purpose, does not reach beyond his coffin; it does not go beyond the purely material world. Steeped in matter, he sees all his happiness in the animal use of the world, and if he is an idealist he may think about science and art.

Surely this is not sufficient for a man, whose thought penetrates the atmosphere and rushes by the stars in the skies, whose intellect is constantly eager to know the causes, to reach up to the First Cause and final purpose of all things, whose heart is eager to possess glory, happiness—the more it attains, the more it desires and feels that nothing limited, not even the most prodigious good, can satiate it. It desires the good, but the infinite good! Let us ask ourselves whether we want to restrict our happiness with the shackles of boundaries? And these people with so narrow a mind, drowned in the gross materialism of our time, dare to prophesy to mankind—happiness? Or maybe they will manage by material means to make mankind happy? Maybe they will cover everyone with gold, surround them with fame, and give them the opportunity to enjoy all kinds of pleasure?

<u>Illusion of morbid imagination</u>. I have already pointed out that what the world can give is not enough for man. All these goods have their limits; they disappoint and awaken the desire for a greater, more permanent happiness, and when this he finds not, man experiences a glut and boredom, and a kind of obscurity envelops the soul. He feels that he was misled on the road to happiness—to the extent that he is still able to reflect on this.

But if only socialism were able to provide, until satiety, this good land—yet it does not.

Liberty, equality, fraternity—they are fine principles, but socialism, after violating human nature, which wishes for wider horizons and tends to infinity, is incapable of providing them; they are too noble and too high.

<u>Liberty</u>. Socialism abolishes private property, or at least the ownership of the means of production. The government, therefore, determines the work, the government evaluates it, the government gives the pay. And this is supposed to be freedom. Here I am

reminded of a conversation with a peasant in Zakopane. Returning from Russian captivity, he was enthused about Bolshevik principles—go and take from the rich. But when I asked him what would happen then with his strip of land, he reasoned that he would cultivate it. "And if you don't want to work?" I asked. "Then the others are obliged to, coerce..." (here he paused), "but I prefer my little patch of land and to be able to do when, what, and how I like with it, rather than obey the one who would become the head of it."

This is an innate desire for freedom that socialists, in the name of freedom!, want to crush.

<u>And equality</u>? We are all equal before God, because we are all His handiwork. All are redeemed by the blood of the God-Man. We all have this God as our ultimate end; we all live only to give Him proof of our fidelity and thereby deserve to possess him forever after death. In all this there is equality. But is it possible on earth to have equality in every respect? Only if we could all be together at the same time, in the same (exact) place and under the same conditions, such as of nature and the environment, would it be possible. But this is physically impossible. We differ in age, birthplace, abilities, inclinations, health, industriousness, foresight, and the events and activities of our lives. All of this comes from the nature of things; consequently, this cannot be changed. There must also be parents and children, superiors and subordinates.

<u>Brotherhood</u>, the noble brotherhood, so sincerely recommended by Christ Our Lord. Could it flourish in socialism? I have here, at hand, a report of a correspondent, the "Courier of Warsaw" from Sopot, who writes, among other things, that "the local Russian cabarets are tailored to the public, which does not count the pennies. For them there are fresh lobsters, iced pineapples and peaches in champagne, grapes, sweets, ice cream in a hot punch. And the public? In these Russian cabarets there must be a public who knows the language. So these are predominantly Jews. At the better tables and bottles at the bar—are the Bolsheviks. In Gdansk, brand new suits, with a Bolshevik star on the lapel, and on a finger, a large signet ring with the engraving of the candlestick of Solomon... Soviet dignitaries, at Sopot, do not count the pennies. They

flee, for a respite, from the cities strewn with corpses of people who have died of starvation—and after they steal the treasures of the Orthodox Church, they throw money at games, champagne, and every amusement."

And there is also a passage from a letter from Odessa printed in the *Journal Wołyń*: "So what if earnings are 300,000 rubles per day, if 40 pounds of flour costs 12,000,000, wheat flour 20,000,000, a pound of bread 300,000, white bread 500,000, a pound of butter 1,500,000, one of lard 1,500,000, eggs 100,000 each, etc. The epidemic is assuming dreadful proportions. In the past sometimes corpses of people who died of starvation would remain for a few days on the sidewalks...now beside these are lying the corpses of those who died of cholera, typhus, the bubonic plague, etc. And the people are buried in the ground like dogs, naked, because the cheapest rough-sawn coffin costs 10,000,000 rubles. Your children are looking forward to You, they want to make their way, to fly to the homeland. But the Soviet's heavy hand holds firmly between his fingers large, sharp scissors, which cut the wings that are looking forward to flight. We all contracted typhus, and as you know, after you have this severe disease you need to eat properly, but where can one obtain the means to do this? In any case the return of typhus awaits us, and we know what it brings with it: death. But I prefer a death caused by an infectious disease, when a man dies with a fever, to the slow agony of starvation..."

Will this be the fraternity and equality proclaimed by the Bolsheviks? Will this be Marx's dream-of paradise?

The path does not lead that way.

It must be recognized that the working class has been in large part disregarded, that socialism has [seemingly] taken up its defense, but one must deplore that it has struck the Church, trying to snatch from the laborer and even a child the most precious treasure of the Faith and the most sublime and innate ideals. Having begun on such a wrong path, it generates only slavery and tyranny of the government over its citizens, and it fails to recognize the aspirations of human nature in its nobility and freedom.

However, these deviations are not something accidental; they are the methodic workings of the "brothers" of the hammer and trowel, who exploit every opportunity to fulfill the motto adopted in 1717: "Destroy all religion, especially Christianity."

Social relationships can be developed and improved. Many things need to be rectified, but this rectification will never be achieved in a manner incompatible with truth and human nature.

With such information, is it still necessary to answer the question, Why does the Church prohibit her children from being socialists?

Rycerz Niepokalanej

40. Who Is God?

[Rycerz Niepokalanej, February 1923, pp. 21–23]

(On this subject I have often spoken, and now I cannot accurately differentiate the thread of the individual conversations; so those parties involved, forgive me, for giving here the debated issue strictly according to a logical connection.)

The darkness increasingly dispersed as the light more abundantly poured its rays through the windows of our carriage on the Grodno-Bialystok-Warsaw line. I had for travel companions, this time, three Jews, quite intelligent. It was possible to recognize them merely by their speech. I initiated a conversation about religion and God. Everyone acknowledged the existence of a First Cause of the universe.

—But who is this Almighty God, this First Cause? - I asked.

—In my opinion - said one of them, whose ordered cheeks and clothing showed quite a comfortable financial position - God is the entirety of nature.

—That cannot be.

—And why not?

—For the simple reason that a cause exists before its effect; therefore, as a consequence of the fact that its existence begins later, it cannot be the same thing as its cause, but must be in reality distinct from it. And so with nature—nature is an effect, and therefore it cannot at the same time be the cause.

—The forces of nature can still be called God.

—Not even that, because these forces are an effect.

—How can we know that these forces are an effect, and not the First Cause?

—Because they are finite.

—So the First Cause must be infinite?

—Undoubtedly.

—Why?

—Whatever exists must have some sort of reason for existence, as well as limits in that existence; it must have its "why." So, in fact, that which is the First Cause cannot be the reason (the "why") for the limits, because whence would they originate? Either from without or from within the First Cause. Not from within, because surely it is first necessary to exist in order to act, and therefore also to limit, and that First Cause which exists is either limited already or not. It cannot draw the boundaries of its essence. Nor could such limits have come from without, because otherwise that cause would not be the first. So neither from within nor from without can there be reason for limitation, and thus such limitation cannot be; this First Cause must therefore be infinite. Everything upon which the mark of limitation is impressed cannot be the First Cause of all things; and surely the forces of nature operate according to laws, which can be grasped in strict mathematical formulas and beyond which these forces do not reach.

—In any case, we cannot know much about God.

—Indeed, it is true that we cannot explore the depths of His essence and His perfection, because God is an infinite being, and our head has limits and fits into a hat; yet, we can know much about Almighty God.

—For example?

—First, we see the purposeful structuring of the members in the human body and in animals and of the parts of plants; in general, we see the intentional harmony in the universe. Therefore, the Being who called all of this into existence must have reason, must be a Person. Then, whatever is in the effect, must in some more perfect manner be in the cause. Consider a painter. He does not give his picture either the paint or the canvas from himself; all this he takes from without. However, what he gives, i.e., the shape, he must have in himself. He first had to imagine the picture before he took a brush into his hand; and according to the model, formed in his mind and in his imagination, he paints. However, Almighty God took nothing from without; He, as the First Cause, brought His creation out of nothing. He gave it everything, and therefore all the perfections of creatures must be in Him—but, as previously indicated, in a manner infinitely perfect, because in Him there can be no limitation.

They listened with interest, and the conversation moved on to the Messiah and the redemption of man.

M. K.

41. The Lenten Fast

[Rycerz Niepokalanej, March 1923, pp. 33–35]

In Zakopane a lady, who was a university student, brought me the pamphlet, well known in Kraków, of Mr. William Rose on the YMCA [Young Men's Christian Association] and, recalling my critique in this regard, she said to me, "I do not see anything wrong with it."

I took the pamphlet and briefly looked through it.

The author, despite his declaration of leaving dogmatic matters to "specialists [and] priests," in fact did not leave them. I found there the teaching of forgiveness of sins through prayer and then the claim that the faithful were wrong in the Middle Ages to mortify their bodies.

On this same subject I also had the opportunity to speak with a Protestant pastor in the city of Nieszawa. He shuddered (as in general the Protestants do) in the face of penance, and regarding St. Paul's admission that "I chastise my body and submit it into slavery, lest perhaps when I have preached I myself should be condemned," he said only that St. Paul practiced it himself, and others are not obliged to imitate him.

Many also in our time want to abolish mortification, because the degraded world of today seeks happiness in temporal, sensual, and often sinful pleasures.

Nevertheless, penance is not the exclusive privilege of St. Paul or an "error" of the Middle Ages, but rather a duty and a *strict duty for all*, because no one is without sin. And not only the "medieval" centuries began to "err," because from the first centuries of the Church the faithful, obedient to the commands of Christ the Lord, kept their bodies under restraint.

Christ the Lord Himself fasted for forty days in the desert and ordered penance under threat of perdition. "If you do not do penance you will all perish together" (Lk 13:5). And St. Peter teaches in the temple, "*Be penitent* and be converted, that your sins may be blotted out" (Acts 3:19).

The first Christians also performed penitential acts, and even the Lenten fast was already known to them. It is mentioned by St. Augustine (†430), St. John Chrysostom (†407), Origen (†253), and St. Irenaeus (†202). They urge the faithful to fervently observe the Lenten fast and condemned those who did not keep it according to the austerity of that time—and certainly it was not yet the Middle Ages.

So everyone who wants to be saved must do penance.

Although Holy Church cannot completely abolish penance, by virtue of the power received from Christ the Lord, she determines how to do penance in regard to the time and place.

One such means of penance is the current *Lenten fast*. In the first centuries it was more brief, but in compensation was significantly more severe. The *Didascalia Apostolorum* (third century) prescribed fasting, i.e., complete abstinence from food and drink, on

Friday and Saturday of Holy Week, and on the four preceding days, fasting on bread, water, and salt. In the beginning of the fourth century, according to the example of the fast of Our Lord Jesus, there was fasting for forty days; the Council of Nicaea had already called this fast (in canon 5) *quadragesima*, the fortieth. In the West, there were six weeks of fasting (Sundays excluded), while in the East (Antioch, Constantinople) there was the custom of excluding from the fast also Saturdays, and thus the fast began seven weeks before Easter. So already there were over thirty days of fasting.

In the seventh century in Rome the number of days of fasting was rounded to forty, beginning with the fast of Ash Wednesday. This custom spread throughout the Catholic world in the beginning of the Middle Ages. Pope Urban II at the Council of Benevento also commanded the whole Church to keep the already old custom of sprinkling ashes on the head at the beginning of the fast. [...]

✻ ✻ ✻

We, members of the Militia of the Immaculata, ought the more fervently to observe (as far as possible) this holy fast, because mortification is a force that together with prayer gains God's grace, purifies the soul, enflames it with love for God and neighbor, and lovingly conquers the soul for God through the Immaculata.

Rycerz Niepokalanej

42. THE BLESSED VIRGIN MARY'S MEDIATION

[*Rycerz Niepokalanej*, March 1923, pp. 45–46]

An international Catholic press agency reports from Brussels that Cardinal Mercier has ordered his pastoral letter to be read in all the churches of his archdiocese; the letter, among other things, says the following:

"Together with the religious congregations, with the theological faculty at Louvain, with the clergy and bishops that have asked God for it and on January 12, 1921, received it, i.e., the ecclesiastical office in honor of Mary as Mediatrix of all graces in the work of redemption. Pope Benedict XV has permitted the Office and Holy Mass in all those dioceses and religious congregations that ask for this grace.

"According to our thoughts and our wishes, this was to be a first step toward the solemn proclamation by the highest ecclesiastical authority of our heavenly Mother's universal mediation. In a briefing of November 28, 1922, the Holy Father deigned to inform us that he has decided to nominate three commissions—one in Rome, another one in Spain, and a third in Belgium—that will study the question, Does the universal mediation of the BVM belong to the deposit of revealed truths? Can it be a matter of definition? In consultation with the nuncio we have appointed the Belgian commission, and it has been confirmed by the Holy Father (composed of two professors of theology in Louvain and Fr. Merkelbach, Dominican professor at the Dominican theological school, also in Louvain)." The cardinal calls for prayers for light for the studies undertaken in this matter and a good outcome.

The Militia bases its activities on this truth. We have recourse to the Immaculata, and we are instruments in Her hands, because She distributes all the graces of conversion and sanctification to the inhabitants of this valley of tears. Furthermore, we clearly profess this truth in the act of consecration to the Blessed Virgin Mary, as it appears in the diplomas [certificates] of the Militia "...since through Thy hands all graces flow to us from the Most Sweet Heart of Jesus."

But on what basis?

Let us look at history. There is not a conversion where in one manner or another Mary's hand was not at work; there is not a saint who was not inflamed by particular devotion to and love for Her.

The Church Fathers and the Doctors have proclaimed that She, the second Eve, has repaired what the first ruined, that She is the channel of divine graces, that She is our hope and refuge, that through Her we receive grace from God. The Holy Father, Pope Leo XIII, in his encyclical on the Rosary (September 22, 1891), says, "It can be affirmed that from that abundant treasure of graces that the Lord brought us...nothing is given to us except through Mary, since God so willed."

Let us pray, therefore, that our Most Holy Mother may hasten the moment of the solemn proclamation of this Her privilege, so that all mankind may run to Her feet with full confidence, for today we are in much need of Her protection.

43. November 27

[Rycerz Niepokalanej, November 1923, pp. 161–165
Republished in Kalendarz Rycerza Niepokalanej 1 (1925), pp. 52–57]

[...] But the actual revelation of the Miraculous Medal falls on November 27. Sr. Catherine describes it thus: "On November 27, the Saturday before the first Sunday of Advent, in the evening while I was making a meditation among deep silence, it seemed to me as if I heard the rustle of a silk dress, which came to me from the right side of the sanctuary, and I saw the Blessed Virgin by the image of St. Joseph; She was of medium height, but of such an extraordinary beauty that it is impossible to describe. She was in a standing position, dressed in a reddish glittering white robe, such that virgins usually wear, i.e., buttoned to the neck and with narrow sleeves. Her head was covered with a white veil, falling to the feet on both sides. Her forehead was graced with a small lace band, adhering tightly to Her hair. Her face was rather uncovered; under Her feet was an earthly globe, or rather half a globe, because I saw only half of it. Her hands, raised up to the waist, gently held another globe (symbol of the whole universe). She raised Her eyes to heaven as if making an offering to Almighty God of the whole universe; Her face shone with ever more brightness.

"There suddenly appeared on Her fingers precious rings studded with gems; from these came forth, in all directions, rays of light, which enveloped Her with such brightness that Her face and dress became invisible. The gems were of different size, and the rays coming forth from them were more or less luminous.

"I cannot express all that I felt and experienced in that short time.

"While I was dazzled with the view of the Blessed Virgin Mary, still gazing on Her majesty, the Blessed Virgin set Her gracious eyes upon me, and an inner voice told me, '*The globe, you see, represents the whole world and each person in particular.*'

"I cannot describe here the impression that I experienced at the sight of the wonderful luminous rays. Then the Blessed Virgin said to me, '*The rays that you see flowing from my hands are a symbol of the graces that I pour out upon those who ask me for them,*' and She enabled me to understand how generous She is to those who have recourse to Her...how many graces She bestows on all those who call upon Her... At that moment I lost self-consciousness, being wholly sunk in happiness... Then the Blessed Virgin, who had returned Her hands so that they pointed toward the ground, was encircled by an oblong circular ring, and on it was an inscription in gold letters: *O Mary conceived without sin, pray for us who have recourse to Thee.*

"Then I heard a voice saying to me, '*Make an effort to have a medal struck according to this model; all those who will wear it will obtain great graces, especially if they wear it around their neck. Upon those who place their trust in me I will bestow many graces.*'

"At that moment," the sister continues, "it seemed to me that the image was rotating. Then I saw on the other side a letter M with a cross that rose from its center, and below the monogram of the Blessed Virgin—were the Heart of Jesus surrounded by a crown of thorns and the Heart of Mary pierced by a sword."

Sr. Catherine saw for the third time the Immaculate Virgin in December of that year. But this time the Blessed Virgin stood over the tabernacle. Around Her could be seen the golden inscription,

"O Mary conceived without sin, pray for us who have recourse to Thee." Above Her appeared the design of the other side of the medal, i.e., the letter M with a cross over the two hearts of Jesus and Mary. The Most Holy Mother again recommended that she make an effort to have a medal struck, according to the indicated model.

The narrative of this apparition she concludes thus: "It is impossible to express what I experienced, when the Blessed Virgin was offering to God the whole world, as well as what I felt when gazing at Her. Again I heard the inner voice: *These rays are a symbol of the graces that the Blessed Virgin obtains for those who ask Her for them.*"

Then, anticipating the great honor that the Blessed Virgin Mary Immaculate will receive from all, Sr. Catherine spontaneously and loudly exclaimed, "Oh how nice, how nice it would be to hear: *Mary is Queen of the whole world*. And all Her children will repeat: *She is the Queen of each one of us*."

Rycerz Niepokalanej

44. Without "Clearer Proofs"

[Rycerz Niepokalanej, January 1924, pp. 3–4]

—He no longer will convert - lamented a dying lady.

I consoled her, as best I could, saying that the Most Holy Mother is able to save hardened sinners, and therefore her husband could be converted.

Soon he came to his wife. A quarrel with the chauffeur was the herald of his arrival. He was a young clerk, a former law student at the university, but in matters of religion very backward, or as it is contrariwise commonly called, "progressive." As a hospital chaplain I thought it my duty, in a certain sense, to also take care of this poor soul. Therefore in free moments I willingly spoke to him about matters pertaining to the Faith. However, the final argument for him was, "I need clearer proofs." I gave him a book by Fr. Morawski that was well known among the intelligentsia: *Evenings on Lake Leman*.

But I noticed that he read little from it; he kept it as some immoral publication. And when I spoke more strongly, he openly declared, "Father, I am a heretic."

I saw that he did not want to be instructed and despised good reading. What to do? I recommended the entire matter to the Immaculata through the intercession of the sanctity of the virgin Gemma Galgani of Lucca, recently deceased and already famous all over the world.

Soon I learn that he leaves the next day, and then I find out that the departure will take place that very night. To make matters worse, one of his relatives came and stayed with him.

In order to have him alone, I had told him that later I would be busy, therefore if he wished to see me, let him do it immediately. And—he came.

From afar I directed the conversation to confession, but heavily it went, till suddenly the door opened, and there was precisely that relative insisting that it is already time to go. So after a brief farewell they left.

I remained alone... How is it possible, I say to myself, that this is the end of this matter?... I fell on my knees and briefly, but fervently, implored the Immaculata through Gemma.

Suddenly, I had an inspiration—I go out into the corridor. I find that relative there.

—Excuse me - I say, turning to him - I need to settle one more thing with that gentleman.

—Yes of course, please - he replied.

My "heretic" had already left the room with suitcase in hand, so I asked him to come over. When the door was closed, I took out a Miraculous Medal and gave it to him as a keepsake. Out of courtesy he accepted it. Then I suggested—that he make a confession.

—I'm not prepared. No. Absolutely not - I heard in reply. But... at that very moment he fell on his knees, as though some higher power compelled him to do so. The confession began.

And he wept like a child...

The Immaculata had won and without "clearer proofs."

Glory to Her forever!

M. K.

45. About the Militia of the Immaculata

[Rycerz Niepokalanej, January 1924, pp. 1–3]

More and more often we receive readers' letters with the request to familiarize them more with the Militia of the Immaculata—so let me say a few words about it.

It was founded in Rome in 1917 among seminarians of the International Franciscan College (Via S. Teodoro 41 F). The occasion for its founding was the increasingly overt actions of Freemasons and other enemies of Christ's Church in the very capital of Christianity; the basis of it was the traditional devotion of the Franciscans, reaching to the cradle of the Order, to the Immaculate Conception. Specific also to the Order was the spirit of poverty, based not so much on the calculations of incomes and expenditures but rather on relying on divine Providence thorough the Immaculata and providing for each one according to his needs—this was the financial basis, the Immaculata's will—the signpost.

On January 2, 1922, the Militia obtained canonical erection by the Cardinal Vicar of Rome; in Poland, the first canonical erection took place recently in Poznan.

The Militia's spirit is summarized briefly in the *MI Program*, which we usually place at the end of every issue of *Knight of the Immaculata*. The letters *MI* come from the Latin name of the Militia of the Immaculata, *Militia Immaculatae*, and serve as an international acronym.

Two sentences placed at the beginning of the program—*She shall crush thy head* (Gn 3:15) and *Thou alone hast destroyed all heresies throughout the world* (Office of the BVM)—are also the Militia's purpose. That is why MI members dedicate themselves to the Immaculata unreservedly as instruments in Her hand, so that through them She may deign to accomplish what is said of Her in these sentences.

At present, Freemasonry is undoubtedly the head of the infernal serpent. I do not say Freemasons because they are unhappy people, but rather I refer to their tendencies, their organization aimed against God and the happiness of souls—*She shall crush thy head.*

The many diverse heresies are the limbs of the serpent. And all of these, and *throughout the world*, She has destroyed, providing reliable measures to eliminate them. And here again, it is not written as "heretics" but "heresies" that She has destroyed; heretics She loves and very much loves like the best Mother, and that is why She saves them from the darkness of falsehood and the evil fetters of the crushing powers of hell. So our aim is "Seek the conversion of sinners, heretics, schismatics, etc., and especially Freemasons, and the sanctification of all under the patronage of *and through the Immaculata*"—yes indeed, the sanctification of all and this under the patronage of and through the Immaculata. Hence, the essence of the MI is the total, unlimited, and unconditional dedication of oneself to the Immaculata as Her property, so that She may deign to do with us whatever pleases Her and act through us in others (an act of such a consecration is, together with the program, in the diploma).

The second condition, or rather the outward sign of this dedication to the Immaculata, in life, death, and eternity—is *Her Miraculous Medal*, which MI members wear on their chests.

Becoming in this way an instrument in the Immaculata's hands, they pray every day with ardent fervor to Her the words that She revealed on the Miraculous Medal: "O Mary conceived without sin, pray for us who have recourse to Thee," and remembering those for whom they desire salvation, they add, "and for all who do not have recourse to Thee, especially the Freemasons." Finally, they also add others whose conversion particularly resides in their heart, either specifically or generally—e.g., "and for those recommended to Thee," including in this way all who at any time commended themselves to their prayer, were mentioned in the *Knight*, etc. This is the power of a prayer that from thousands of hearts every day soars to the Immaculata.

Besides prayer, there is an occupation. It varies according to each one's conditions and circumstances, animated by eagerness and directed by prudence. However, the common characteristic of this work is to draw souls, as many souls as possible, toward the Immaculata. She will cleanse them of their sins, enlighten and strengthen them, and enkindle in them the love of the Heart of Jesus and their neighbors. She will make them happy—as the saints rightly say, <u>it is impossible for the one who honors Mary to perish</u>: "love toward the Most Holy Mother is a sign of predestination."

And as the Immaculata promised to grant many graces to those who will wear Her medal, MI members use it as a bullet in the battle to gain souls for the Immaculata, certain that the more sincerely and profoundly the reign of the Immaculata takes possession of the world, the more it will be transformed into—a <u>paradise on earth</u>. Currently, the *Knight of the Immaculata* is a link between MI members scattered all over Poland.

[...] Let everyone enlist under the Immaculata's banner.

Rycerz Niepokalanej

Masonic journal

46. The Immaculata's Orders

[Rycerz Niepokalanej, February 1924, pp. 17–19]

Who has not heard about the apparitions of the Immaculata at Lourdes, the authenticity of which is attested by numerous miracles.

As in various epochs of the life of mankind, so also in our time, such as in 1858, the Immaculata has extended a hand to Her children, perishing in the depths of unbelief and immorality. The current month is the anniversary of that memorable moment. She recommended two things to all of us.

✻ ✻ ✻

[...] In the grotto appeared a Lady of marvelous beauty. [...] She held her hands devoutly, and in them—was the <u>Holy Rosary</u>.

Bernadette fell on her knees and took out her rosary. The Lady of the apparition slowly and devoutly crossed herself. Bernadette does the same and begins to recite the Creed and Our Father, and then the Hail Mary, one after another. The beautiful Lady moves also the white beads of Her rosary, but Her lips remain motionless. Just as Bernadette finished the last Glory be, the Lady disappeared. This was on February 11.

※ ※ ※

[...] On February 23, She ordered her to tell the priests that She wishes a chapel to be built for Her at the grotto. [...] The apparition is repeated the next day, and Bernadette herself told the pastor about it:

"[...] She told me to pray for sinners and ordered me to enter inside the cave, and exclaimed three times: <u>*Penance! Penance! Penance!*</u>, and I repeated these words, crawling on my knees to the center of the grotto. [...]"

And despite the ridicule of the "philosophers" and the "learned" of Lourdes, and even the violence of the secular authorities, the apparition recurred. A spring that healed the sick already abandoned by doctors as incurable rose up miraculously. On the solemnity of the Annunciation of the Blessed Virgin Mary, the Lady appeared for the last time. Bernadette, imbued with happiness, asked,

—O my Lady, be so good as to tell me who You are and what Your name is.

The Apparition only smiled, and Bernadette continued to ask:

—O my Lady, be so kind as to tell me who You are and what Your name is.

The marvelous Lady brightened even more, but answered nothing. Bernadette, however, further insisted:

—O my Lady, be so good as to tell me who You are and what Your name is.

Lourdes grotto that Kolbe built behind the Japanese friary

A heavenly light more fully surrounded the beautiful Lady, but there was no response. Bernadette, however, still insists.

Then the heavenly Lady opened Her joined hands, placed Her rosary upon Her right hand, extended both hands, tilting them toward the earth, then raised them again, then folded them and, looking up to heaven with inexpressible gratitude, said,

—I AM THE IMMACULATE CONCEPTION - and disappeared.

[...] Prayer, therefore, and especially the *Rosary* and *penance*— here are the Immaculata's orders for us all.

47. Why Do the Good Suffer?

[Rycerz Niepokalanej, February 1924, pp. 19–20]

Only the day before yesterday someone asked me this question:
—The good in general suffer, and the evil are often doing well. Where is the justice in this?
—Almighty God is infinitely just, is it not true?
—Yes, so it is.
—Otherwise, He would not be God. Therefore, Almighty God must give recompense for every good deed and punishment for every evil deed. No action, no word, no thought will escape His judgment. Now, is there in the world a man, even the worst sort, who has never done something good?
—No, there is no such man.
—Every man will sometimes fulfill his obligations well, or exhibit mercy toward his neighbor, or something else that is good. Now if that man leads such an evil life that after death he merits hell, when will Almighty God repay him for the little good he has done?... When?...
—In the next world.
—But only hell awaits him there.
—Well, in this world...

—Now then, is there any man, even the best, who has never done anything wrong?

—No, there is no such man.

—That is correct, for even the just man falls "seven times a day." Therefore if Almighty God wishes to shorten his stay in purgatory or to give him entry into heaven at once, when will the books be balanced?

—Oh, that's so...

—Almighty God shows particular love to those whom He punishes already in this world, because in purgatory there is only punishment both long and severe, and in this world by the voluntary acceptance of crosses we merit an even greater glory in heaven; hence the proverb, "whom God loves, He chastises."

Therefore, do not be envious of these evil people, who prosper; indeed they should greatly fear that this already could be the recompense for the little good that they have done.

M. K.

48. I Am an Unbeliever

[Rycerz Niepokalanej, March 1924, pp. 44–45]

(Based on a conversation with a university student in December 1920.)

—I am an unbeliever.

—That means?

—I do not believe.

—But in what?

—What the priests say.

—For example?

—Here: they just had celebrated the Immaculate Conception. How is it possible that the Mother of God had no father?

—What is the Immaculate Conception?

—That the Mother of God like Our Lord Jesus came down from heaven into the world.
—Sir, you are not an unbeliever, but one who does not know.
—And why is that?
—Because the Immaculate Conception is something completely different; it means that the Immaculate Virgin, coming into the world, from the first moment of Her conception, was free from original sin. How is it possible not know that!?...

M. K.

49. Does Truth Change?

[Rycerz Niepokalanej, April 1924, pp. 55–57]

It was March 13 of this year. I was riding to Warsaw. Opposite me sat a good-natured Jewish woman. Beside her was a lad who was also of the Mosaic confession, while on his right was an intelligent lady whose origin was indicated only by her immersion in a newspaper of an incomprehensible language. I finished my breviary and glanced at the daily, and I invoked the Immaculata. I was seeking an opportunity to start a conversation. I turned finally to the youngster.
—Are you an Israelite?
—Yes, that's right.
—And from what political faction?
—I'm a Zionist.
—Could you then explain the goals of Zionism?
—You must know them already.
—Yes, I've heard many things about Zionism, but I would like to learn about it from the lips of a Zionist.

The intelligent individual, who evidently shared the views of the youngster, entered the conversation, arguing that the goal of Zionists is to regain their homeland for the dispersed Jews.
—But you all cannot dwell in Palestine - I noted - so surely Zionism has drawn itself a more extensive plan?

They argued that it did not [1], then they distinguished between Zionists as "progressive" and the orthodox as "devout," "clerical."

—And which of them is right? - I asked.

—One cannot establish the truth, for it changes with time - claimed this lady - so, e.g., before it was true that the sun revolves around the earth, and now after Copernicus it is true that it is the earth that revolves around the sun, and we do not know how it will be later. Therefore, the truth is variable.

—Madam, how much is two plus two?

—Four.

—And how much was it a hundred years ago?

—Also four.

—And how much will it be in one thousand years?

—...The same, of course, but this is only applicable to mathematical truths.

—Is the whole greater or smaller than a part?

—Obviously, it is always greater, but that is a mathematical truth. Consider, however, this matter: we say that this paper is white, and yet color is an impression related to our sight.

—Madam, if you please, it is one thing to explain what the color white is and quite another to say whether this paper is white. In the first case, we point to the causes of the matter, and obviously we cannot at once make theorems without adequate study. It is good, also, to distinguish between things that are certain, very probable, probable, and doubtful. Thus, e.g., the current theory or hypothesis for the vibrations of ether, the reflections and refractions of its rays, etc., are indeed very probable, although no scientist dares to declare it yet as an axiom of science. It is otherwise with the fact of the matter that this paper is white. Here we have absolute certainty, without entering completely into explanations of what its whiteness consists in and how it happens that we see this paper as white. This also relates to your example of the movement of the earth around the sun. And today, it is no surprise when an astronomer, having studied the starry sky all night, at dawn looks at the resplendent horizon and says, "How beautiful is the sunrise!" Indeed, it would sound far more odd if, not expressing direct observation, he said, "O how beautiful, the earth revolves around the sun!" The saying "the sun rises" probably is now and will always be the same, although the reasons for that phenomenon can be variable, as long as there is no absolute certainty.

—And what other sort of truths are there?

—For example, that we are sitting here and conversing. That is a truth and will remain such forever.

—But afterward we will leave here; therefore that truth will change.

—Not at all, for it will remain true forever that at this time we sat here and held a conversation. And even if all the people in the world claimed and swore and, if they wished, sang in four or in ten voices that it was not so, despite it all they would be telling an untruth, because this incident will remain true.

M. K.

[1] Though not all Jews know this, the founders of Zionism were actually interested in mastery over the world. A major piece of evidence for this is the *Protocols of the Elders of Zion* (Perzynski Bookstore, Nowy Swiat 21, Warsaw). And this reduces the workings of Freemasonry.

50. Body of the Lord

[Rycerz Niepokalanej, June 1924, pp. 98–100]

On the 19th of this month, the workshops will stop operating, manual labor will subside, and crowds of the faithful and many curious, though non-Catholic, people will participate in the magnificent annual Corpus Christi procession. There will be many beautiful hymns, music, and perhaps also rifle salvos. [...]

❈ ❈ ❈

It was in Capernaum, a town by the Sea of Galilee. Crowds gathered around Our Lord Jesus, and He, among other things, said to them, "I am the living bread, which came down from heaven; he who eats this bread will live forever; and the bread that I will give is my Flesh for the life of the world." When the Jews, having literally understood the Savior's words, asked, "How can this man give us his Flesh to eat?," Christ Our Lord solemnly emphasized the literalness of his words: "Amen, amen, I say to you: if you do not eat the Flesh of the Son of Man and drink His Blood, you shall not have life in you. He that eats my Flesh and drinks my Blood hath everlasting life, and I will raise him up in the last day. For my Flesh is food indeed and my Blood is drink indeed. He that eats my Flesh and drinks my Blood, dwelleth in me, and I in him. As the living Father has sent me, and I live by the Father, so he that eats me shall live because of me. This is the bread that came down from heaven! Not as your fathers did eat manna and died; whoever eats this bread shall live forever."

This promise of the Savior the apostle St. John heard also with his own ears, and he recorded it in his Gospel (Jn 6:51–60).

Six months later at Jerusalem in the Upper Room, the Apostles gathered around the Savior to eat the Passover lamb. It was the last supper, the moment of separation, precisely in which the Savior decided to fulfill the promise he made half a year earlier. "And while they were at supper," says St. Matthew, who was present, "Jesus took bread and blessed and broke it, and gave it to His disciples and said: *Take and eat—this is my Body*. And taking the chalice, he gave thanks and gave it to them, saying: *Drink ye all of this; for this is my Blood of the New Covenant, which shall be shed for many, unto the forgiveness of sins*" (Mt 26:26–28). And He added, as affirmed by St. Luke (22:19) and St. Paul (1 Cor 11:24–25), "Do this in remembrance of me."

And from that moment the Holy Sacrifice of the Mass was established on earth, offered ever more frequently, and becoming more and more widespread—at first underground in the catacombs, later in more and more churches.

And on June 19 a priest, a successor [to the successors] of the Apostles, obedient to the command of the God-Man, repeats in His memory the moving scene of the Last Supper. The bread becomes the living Body of Christ, and the wine—His most precious Blood.

And He, the Creator of heaven and earth and Redeemer of souls, comes out into the paths and streets where His children walk, carried in the hands of a priest. [...]

The aged Simeon, holding in his hands the expected Messiah, prophesied, "Behold this is set for the fall...of many in Israel: and for a sign that shall be contradicted." [...]

Rycerz Niepokalanej

51. Papal Infallibility

[*Rycerz Niepokalanej*, June 1924, pp. 101–103]

—I won't say that I'm an unbeliever; I believe in the existence of God, but then again, it is impossible to acknowledge as truth everything that the Catholic Church teaches.

—And why is that?

—Because certain things do not agree with the facts.

—For example?

—Not long ago papal infallibility was declared as a dogma, and yet it is not possible to say that all Popes have never strayed from the right path.

—So you wish to say, that the Pope can sin?

—That's right.

—Nobody denies that. Indeed, I can assure you that the Pope also confesses and as frequently as any other devout person, that is, weekly. I even know personally a priest who was a confessor to the late Holy Father, Benedict XV. He is Fr. Alexander Basile, a Jesuit. Therefore we should distinguish *infallibility* from *impeccability*.

—Still, even in that sense I would not call the Pope infallible. For how can one assume that the Pope, because he is Pope, possesses already all knowledge and is able to correctly answer every question?

—But sir, you have probably never read about the dogma of papal infallibility. Nobody demands all this of the Pope. The Pope is infallible only in matters of <u>faith and morals</u>, and not even whenever he speaks or writes on these matters, but only when as <u>shepherd of the entire Church</u>, with his supreme apostolic authority, he solemnly proclaims that a given statement concerning faith or morals is revealed truth, or strictly connected with revealed truths, and that therefore <u>everyone must accept</u> it as such. So the Pope is not in the least infallible in matters related exclusively to natural science, politics, etc., and even in matters of faith and morals when he speaks only as a common priest or scholar. So, e.g., the many works of Pope Benedict XIV, though they have great authority as magnificent works of a scholar, still do not belong to the category of dogma.

In matters of faith and morals, it truly <u>could not</u> be otherwise, for what kind of a Church would we have if nothing is certain, if it is not possible to know what to believe and how to behave? The view of Protestantism fragmenting before our very eyes is the best image of this. For what benefit, then, would be the teaching of Christ Our Lord? How could Our Lord Jesus in such a case threaten with damnation those who do not believe the Apostles (see Mk 16:16), if all can preach falsehood? What would the Savior's words uttered to Peter mean—"I have prayed for thee, that thy faith fail not; and thou then converted thyself <u>confirm</u> thy brethren"—if he were fallible? How could he, then, confirm others? And finally, how would Christ's words to Peter be fulfilled: "Thou art a rock, and upon this rock I will build My church, and the powers of hell shall not prevail against it"? After all, if the Pope taught falsehood or moral evil, falsehood and evil would already be celebrating their triumph.

—So I suppose that Almighty God needs to reveal to the Pope, in such instances, what the truth is?

—That is not at all needed; it is sufficient that Almighty God not allow him to err; after all, dogmatic definitions are preceded by a thorough study by scholars of Sacred Scripture and Church

Tradition reaching back to the first centuries, and only then can the Pope say the last word.

—In any case, in this entire matter there is something extraordinary.

—Obviously, but does not the matter of the salvation of souls deserve that? Moreover, for Almighty God it is not more difficult to perform extraordinary things than those that we call ordinary. Only for us is there such a difference—for things and events that frequently fall under our senses are for us ordinary, and what is rare or what we have never seen is for us extraordinary.

M. K.

52. Victory of the Immaculata

[Rycerz Niepokalanej, August 1924, pp. 148–150]

Recently a lady came to see me and ask if I would go to a sick person, who...did not want to confess. He had already been seen by Fr. H., who had just sent her to me, because his attempts had failed.

—Does he refuse to pray to the Most Holy Mother at least one Hail Mary a day? - I asked.

—I suggested it to him, but he replied that he did not believe in the Mother of God.

—Please take this medal to him - I said, giving her a Miraculous Medal. - Perhaps he will accept it for your sake and allow you to put it around his neck?

—He will accept it to please me.

—Very well, take it to him and pray for him; then I will try to go there to see him.

And she went...

Meanwhile, I met with Fr. H. "I was with the sick person, as with my friend," he told me, "but I could do nothing. Please go there. In addition I must point out that the patient is an intellectual person; just graduated in forestry at the university."

Shortly thereafter, this lady came back to notify me that the patient's condition was worse, and his parents, present beside him, are quite reluctant to send for a priest, because they fear that the priest would not impress him. "The patient doesn't want a priest and his parents also: so why go there?" I thought to myself, but despite everything I went, though deep in my soul a doubt pervaded as to whether the effort would prove successful. My only hope was the medal that the sick person was now wearing. On my way, I prayed the Rosary. After an arduous walk, I rang the hospital's doorbell. Soon I was taken to the room for contagious diseases, where he had been lying ill. I sat beside his bed and started a conversation. I asked about his health, but soon the conversation turned to religious matters. The patient manifested his doubts, and I tried to clarify them for him. During the conversation, I noticed a thin blue cord around his neck, the very one from which the medal was hanging. He has the medal, I thought; therefore, the cause has been won.

Suddenly, the patient turned to me and said,

—Father, could we come to the point?

—So you want to confess? - I asked.

In response, mournful weeping shook his emaciated breast... It lasted a good while... Once the patient calmed down, he began to confess.

After receiving Viaticum and Extreme Unction, the patient, to show his thanks, embraced and kissed me. Despite the risk of contagion, I willingly gave him the kiss of peace. Glory to the Immaculata for this victory!!!

※ ※ ※

Another patient was lying nearby. At the hospital, they told me that death was already near at hand for him; but he was not thinking about confession. So I commended him also to the Immaculata through the intercession of the recently beatified Bl. Thérèse of the Child Jesus. The next day I came as if to visit the previous sick person, but in fact I came for the second. I sat down beside the first patient, but meanwhile I requested that the nurse ask him if he would be willing to take advantage of my presence. The patient had not noticed me. He answered impatiently, "The doctor says that in a week I will recover, and here you are boring me with a priest."

Not discouraged by such a disposition, I began a conversation with him and sat beside him. Seeing that the patient obstinately put off confession, I took out our "bullet" in the Militia, i.e., the Miraculous Medal. The patient asked, "What is it?" I briefly explained to him. He kissed it, allowed it to be put around his neck, and…the confession began.

May there be eternal thanks to the Immaculata for such gracious and merciful victories.

M. K.

53. Does Almighty God Know Everything?

[Rycerz Niepokalanej, November 1924, pp. 219–221]

—I cannot understand how Almighty God can know everything.

—Neither can I.

—So?

—After all, what is contrary to reason cannot be. And such is God's omniscience.

—My dear fellow! If you cannot, as you say, understand how God can know everything, this matter already, strictly speaking (with reasoning, speaking strictly is necessary), is neither contrary nor opposed to your reason.

—I do not understand you now.

—Listen! Could it be true that you are standing here conversing with me, yet also true that you are not here at all?

—If I stand here, I think that I'm here.

—And if someone claimed the contrary, would his claim be contrary to your reason?

—Undoubtedly.

—And why?

—Because I clearly see that this is so, and not otherwise.

—So you clearly see, that is, you realize, that this is contrary to your reason.

—Obviously.

—You see, therefore, that all the certainty that something is contrary to reason certainly does not come from the fact that one does not understand something, but in fact that one sees clearly that it would be absurd to say otherwise. Well, what I'm trying to say is this: precisely because you cannot understand how God knows everything, you cannot know anything about it, much less say anything.

—So we know nothing about it?

—Nothing.

—How is that? After all, the catechism clearly states that Almighty God is omniscient.

—Obviously! But there it only says that Almighty God knows everything, without explaining, and much less determining, how it is so.

—Exactly. But I will tell you where my difficulty is. Well, I've heard, and it must be so, that Almighty God knows all about what I will do in an hour, tomorrow, in the hour of my death, and even if I will be saved or damned. Yet, on the other hand, it depends on me! How then can this be reconciled?

—Here we enter now within the scope of the question, <u>How</u> does Almighty God know everything? In turn, as I said above, we know nothing. So, if anyone says to me that he "understands" how it can be, [that God knows everything], or "understands" that it cannot be, I would say to him plainly that he either mocks me or does not know what it is about. You see, it is about understanding the capability of the Infinite Intellect! Unfortunately, however, our heads, as daily experience teaches us, are often imperfectly, or altogether not at all, familiar with issues of ordinary life. How can we, therefore, dream of a proportion between our notions and God's knowledge, especially when there is an <u>infinite</u> difference here? In vain, e.g., would one strain his mind and inflate his head to know yet how far his intelligence extends into space. He could follow his thought to the moon, pass the sun, reach for the stars, the nebulas and…and…? Thereby he neither discerns the ending…nor understands the beginning! Because yet before him and behind him is more and more…space. Where is the answer to the puzzle? Here it is: <u>we are finite</u>! However despite this you can imagine some resemblance, although distant and very inaccurate, e.g., we are conversing here, right?

—Right.

—And you came here voluntarily?

—No one forced me.

—Do you and I know about this incident?

—Obviously we do.

—After this incident, consider: can one say that we were not here and have not conversed with each other?

—Probably as a joke.

—Thus the knowledge that it was so is certain?

—A miracle cannot make it be what it was not, what already has happened!

—Well said. So you see that <u>after</u> an incident we will have complete certainty that it happened in a specific manner and not otherwise, though, as you say, no one forced you to come here and converse with me. This is how our human knowledge is: finite.

But in the cognition of God, or rather in the knowledge of God, there is a big difference. Since His knowledge is infinite, for Him there actually cannot exist any "before" or "after." Therefore God knows everything <u>always</u>, i.e., at every moment, and thus, humanly speaking, both before and after. But now this cannot fit in our finite head.

M. K.

54. The Cult of the Immaculate Conception [1]

[Kalendarz Rycerza Niepokalanej, 1925, pp. 40–46
RN 11 (1932) pp. 356–361]

It was Paris, the year 1305.

A young friar is leaving a Franciscan convent and, deep in thought, is heading to the most famous university at that time in the world, the Sorbonne. He is thinking about the Immaculata and is invoking Her with interior aspirations, so that She assists him in defending Her privilege, so dear to Her,—the Immaculate Conception. Precisely today, in fact, at the behest of the Pope and in front of his legates, a general hearing is to take place between the supporters of this privilege and its opponents.

And this hearing was caused by him...

Recently he had taken the professorial chair there in place of William Warra, who was retiring because of advanced age. By order of the Father General he had left the university chair in Oxford, where also he had zealously preached about the Immaculate Conception. And from everywhere the students had thronged to him, until their number had reached thirty thousand. Now he had come to Paris. And here he does not fail to defend openly the Immaculate Conception. It was only since November 18 (of 1304) that he moved from Oxford to Paris, and already complaints against him—because he openly preached about the privilege of the Immaculate Conception—had reached Pope Clement V in Avignon. Allegedly he preached a doctrine that was based on an exaggerated devotion to the Blessed Virgin and that was contrary to the Faith. And precisely today, in front of all the professors and even in the presence of the legates of the Pope, he must justify it.

Could he do otherwise? He, a Franciscan, a spiritual son of the holy patriarch of Assisi?...

The holy father Francis... It was he, after all, who upon sending the first brothers to the conquest of souls taught them the prayer to

Our Lady: "Hail Lady...chosen by the Most Holy Father in heaven, whom He consecrated with His Most Holy and Most Beloved Son and with the Holy Spirit, the Comforter. In You is and was all fullness of grace and every good." He had also there in Rovigo, in northern Italy, praised Her Immaculate Conception in the presence of a crowd of listeners and had there collected offerings and built a church dedicated to the Mother of God, and he erected therein an altar to the Conception of the Blessed Virgin. [2] And St. Anthony, one of the first sons of the holy father Francis, does he not call Mary in his sermons by the sweet name of Immaculate Virgin? [3] Now only forty years have passed since the seventh minister general of the Franciscans, St. Bonaventure, ordered at the General Chapter in Pisa (1263) that all the sons of the holy father Francis, all the convents, and all the Provinces celebrate the feast of the Immaculate Conception.

Yes, he is entitled, has a duty, as a Franciscan, to joust in defense of so sublime a privilege of the Mother of God.

Parisian professors claim that it is a new doctrine. It is true that the term may seem new, but actually, wasn't it professed by the faithful from the earliest days of the Church? Didn't they profess it everywhere, proclaiming that She is full of grace, the purest, the most holy? After all, the stain of original sin is precisely the negation of fullness of grace and sanctity.

A new doctrine?... Have not the Church Fathers, clearly enough, proclaimed their belief and that of their centuries in the Immaculate Conception of Mary, claiming that She is the purest in every respect and totally immaculate, the purest, always pure, that in Her sin has never had dominion, that She is more than holy, more than innocent, holy under every aspect, pure without stain, holier than the saints, purer than the heavenly spirits, alone holy, alone innocent, alone immaculate, the one and only immaculate beyond all measure and the one and only blessed beyond all measure?... [4]

The truth is that not all of them thoroughly know the Church Fathers' writings, especially the eastern Fathers; and so—let them read also those parchments.

They say that the affirmation that the Blessed Virgin was free from the stain of original sin is an affront to the dignity of Christ the Lord, who redeemed everyone without exception and died for all. But isn't it precisely for this that by the merits of His future death He did not allow that any stain would defile Her? Isn't it precisely for this that He redeemed Her in the most perfect way? Isn't he who removes a stone from the road so that another person will not trip and fall doing a greater favor than the one who raises those who have already fallen?...

So many different objections I've heard, but no one can resist the criticism.

Yes, Almighty God is able to preserve his Mother even from the stain of original sin. He undoubtedly wanted to do it, for why would He have not willed to do this, for the One who was to be the worthy Mother of an infinitely pure and holy God—and so...He did it?...

Yes, undoubtedly—He did it.

Scotus raises his eyes; he is just passing by a house where from within a door frame the Immaculata is benevolently looking upon him from a statue carved out of marble.

His heart beats with joy. He recalls from his boyhood years, when he had knocked on the door of the Franciscan convent in Oxford, and was accepted, how with great difficulty he had studied from lack of capacity, and having prayed about this to the Immaculate Virgin, Seat of Wisdom, had abundantly received this grace and had promised the Immaculata to devote all his genius and all his knowledge to Her honor.

For Her, precisely, he is going now to fight. He took off his cap and fervently sighed. "Allow me to praise Thee, O Most Sacred Virgin. Give me strength against Thy enemies" [5]. And he saw that the Immaculata with a bow of Her head promised to help him [6]. Filled with gratitude, immersed in his own unworthiness, and inflamed with love toward his Immaculate Lady, he headed onward.

In the large hall of the university, on both sides, sat many opponents of the Immaculate Conception. The modest Scotus took his place and humbly waited for them to give him the floor. Three envoys of the Pope also entered and took their places at the head of the hall, to listen to the dispute and preside over it.

Meanwhile, the opponents came forward. In multiple arguments that numbered as many as two hundred, they thrashed the affirmation of the poor Franciscan.

Finally, the objections exhausted, there was silence. A legate of the Pope gives the floor to Scotus. He, inspiring the greatest awe in the many people present, enumerates all the objections in the same order and very thoroughly refutes them, and then with clear proofs of the Immaculate Conception of the Blessed Virgin, justifies this doctrine. His arguments were so convincing that the professors and scholars present immediately, according to the custom of the time, awarded him a title according to his ability, i.e., subtle [doctor].

Pelbart of Temeswar, a near contemporary of these events, describes the scene this way: "These (who denied the Immaculate Conception) opposed a brilliant doctor. Strong arguments were given against it, and there were two hundred of them. All of them, without interruption, he calmly and confidently, but attentively, listened to, and with amazing memory, in the same order, he repeated them, solving the intricate difficulties and arguments with such ease, as Samson did with the bonds of Delilah. Scotus also added many and very strong arguments, proving that the Blessed Virgin was conceived without the stain of sin. His discourse made such an impression on the scholars of the University of Paris that as a token of recognition they awarded Scotus with the honorable title of Subtle Doctor" [7].

From then on, the Franciscans, scattered across various parts of Europe, with greater boldness proclaimed everywhere to the faithful the Immaculate Conception of the Most Pure Virgin.

* * *

When on November 8, 1308, the brave defender of the privilege of the Immaculate Conception, now in Cologne, left this earthly exile, where he had also, in his last years, taught at a university, the belief in the Immaculate Conception of Mary had already so deeply taken root that an illustrious Spanish theologian, Vasquez, could aptly write in the fifteenth century, "Since the time of Scotus (belief in the Immaculate Conception) so increased, not only among the scholastic theologians but also among the people, that nobody now could manage to obliterate it" (*Hist. Saec.* IV in 3 p.d. 117 cap. 2 ap., Bened. XIV, *De Festis*, lib. II cap. 15).

One hundred and seventy years after the Paris disputation, another dispute took place, lasting several days, in the Vatican, in the presence of the Holy Father Sixtus IV, who was also a Franciscan. The thirty-ninth minister general of the Franciscans, Fr. Francis Nanni, so splendidly dispersed the difficulties presented by the opponents that the impressed Pope exclaimed, "You are indeed a powerful Samson." After that, the Holy Father issued (February 27, 1476) the famous constitution in which he confirmed the Office and Mass of the Immaculate Conception, arranged by Leonard of Nugarolis, and granted an indulgence to all who would assist at the Office or celebrate the Holy Mass, as also to all those present at these, on the feast day or the octave of the Immaculate Conception.

The belief in the Immaculate Conception of the Mother of God became ever more vivid. What formerly was hidden in faith in "fullness of grace," the sanctity and purity of the immaculate Mother of God, was now expressly indicated, specifically venerated, and called by its own name, until the moment, proper according to the judgment of God, when the Holy Father Pius IX, the two hundred and fifty-sixth successor of St. Peter, surrounded by fifty-three cardinals, forty-two archbishops, ninety-two bishops, and countless multitudes of the faithful, as the supreme shepherd of the entire Church, solemnly declared that the doctrine which holds that the Blessed Virgin Mary in the first moment of Her conception was by a special grace and privilege of Almighty God, on account of the merits of Jesus Christ the Savior of mankind, preserved free from all stain of original sin, is revealed by God.

Then the Pope crowned a painting of the Immaculate Conception, which the Franciscan Pope Sixtus IV had placed on the chapel's altar, dedicated to this privilege of the Mother of God.

Four years later, the Immaculata Herself, as if to confirm the proclaimed dogma, declared in Lourdes, "I am the Immaculate Conception."

Niepokalanej Rycerz

[1] In the [original] text there are two illustrations. The first depicts Duns Scotus before a statue of the Immaculata. The caption reads, "Allow me to praise Thee, Most Sacred Virgin. Give me strength against Thy enemies." The second depicts Fr. Francis Nanni before Sixtus IV; caption: "You are indeed a powerful Samson." - editor of the *Pisma sw. Maksymiliana Kolbego*.
[2] Nicolean de Rebus Rhodigin., lib. 2.
[3] *Sermon of Pentecost*.
[4] Testimonies collected accurately from Passaglia in his work *De Immac. Deiparae Conceptu*, parts II and VI.
[5] Over time this invocation was included in the Divine Office.
[6] The statue of the Immaculata with Her head bowed was on display until 1789, when the Masons during the Revolution destroyed it.
[7] Stellar, *BMV*, lib. 4.

55. "Knight of the Immaculata"

[Kalendarz Rycerza Niepokalanej, 1925, pp. 97–98]

[...] THE PURPOSE of "Knight of the Immaculata" is to promote filial love for and confidence in the Immaculate Queen of Heaven and earth, so that this Refuge of Sinners reigns as soon as possible in the hearts of each and every individual. In fact, when that happens the earth will become a paradise. True peace and happiness will come upon the families, cities, villages, and countries of all human societies, because where She reigns, there also the grace of conversion and sanctification, and happiness, will appear.

[...] To hasten the most merciful reign of the Immaculata on earth?

[...] Let the hour strike as quickly as possible in which one could say, THE IMMACULATA IS QUEEN OF ALL AND EVERY INDIVIDUAL.

56. The Same Old Thing

[Rycerz Niepokalanej, January 1925, pp. 1–3]

Amateur philosophers of our day are saying, writing, and publishing many "novelties," and now the one who says something "wise"—such as there is no God, human reason above all else, etc.—calls himself "progressive."

It might seem that this is really something new. Yet by no means. This is as old as the world, and even older.

When there was not yet a man on earth, rebellious Lucifer already had proclaimed, "I will ascend into heaven...I will be like the Most High" (Is 14:13–14). Thus "I," I myself, will ascend up into heaven, and will be...God.

It was the same thing with our first parents in paradise. Having heard from the tempter the promise "You shall be as gods" (Gn 3:5), they allowed themselves to be seduced, sinned by disobedience, and brought misery to the earth.

And our know-it-alls are convinced, or rather they would like to convince themselves, that they, oh, they are standing in an aureole of wisdom and are already demigods, if not fully divine. Reason is idolized; this limited reason found itself, in fact, upon an altar during the French Revolution—personified by a shameless hag. Yet about God they would prefer not to think, not to speak; rather, they mindlessly repeat "there is no God," because...if there were—it would be necessary to live differently.

What is the cause of these downfalls?

Perhaps this very desire and the aspiration to [be like God] is immoral and unwise?

No, because each of us feels this desire in himself and in each and every act aspires to it. It is, therefore, innate, natural. Our nature tends to increasingly improve itself—by degrees...and even, in a certain sense, to seek divinization.

The sacred book also expressly exhorts us to imitate God and become Godlike.

So wherein is the fault?

Almighty God is infinite truth; therefore He cannot withstand untruth, falsehood. On the other hand, man is a creature brought into existence from nothing, and therefore of himself he is nothingness, absolute <u>nothingness</u>. Therefore whatever he has, and is, he has received from God, or rather, in every moment of his life is receiving, for to persevere in existence is to receive existence at every moment, if he is not of himself, as Almighty God is. And all ability of growth, all acquired perfection—all this without the slightest exception originates from <u>that Source of existence</u>. How, then, does the madman look who dares to say that he alone, without divine assistance, will continue to perfect himself, and even reach the summit?! (In being conformed to God we will never reach the summit, because in man there is no infinite perfection.) And what kind of reasoning is it which, seeing that of himself he is nothing, that all he receives is from the outside, makes the statement, "There is no God"??!!!

Only one thing can be said for its partial justification. Reason is eager to know the cause of things; the more keen it is, the further in pursuit of the First Cause it will go. Darkened, however, by an immoral life, or pride, it gets stuck at the very outset; it is not able to go beyond itself, and thence comes the thought that it, itself, has become the alpha and omega of the universe. So this is reason, but a restricted, abnormal reason, or as it is generally preferred to be called—stupid.

Hence the psalmist sings, "The fool said in his heart: there is no God" (Ps 52:1).

Almighty God, as infinite truth, <u>cannot</u> fail to correct such a falsehood; for this He immediately condemned the rebel angels and punished Adam and Eve, and He will not fail to mete out justice to our haughty fools.

※ ※ ※

Let us pray fervently to the Immaculata, to obtain for them the grace of conversion, before the punishing hand of divine justice bears down upon them.

Rycerz Niepokalanej

57. How Should a Knight (or Lady) of the Immaculata Think and Act?

[Rycerz Niepokalanej, February 1925, pp. 25–27]

The blessed month of February has come again. Blessed, because on the 11th we celebrate annually the commemoration of the apparition of the Immaculate Virgin at Lourdes.

How can we worthily celebrate this commemoration?

Let all of us who have enlisted ourselves in the ranks of Her Knights on this day purify our souls from sin and admit into our hearts God, residing in our midst in the Most Blessed Sacrament of the Altar. If anyone is not able on the same day of February 11 to receive Holy Communion sacramentally, let him not omit spiritual communion and let him endeavor at the first opportunity to communicate sacramentally.

Secondly, let us look, today, at the image of a true Knight and Lady of the Immaculata.

He does not confine his heart to himself alone, nor to his family, relatives, friends, neighbors, fellow countrymen, but rather he embraces within it the whole world, all and every individual, because they are all, without exception, redeemed by the Blood of Our Lord Jesus; all are our brethren. For all he desires true happiness and enlightenment in the light of faith; he wants all to be cleansed from sin; he wants their hearts to be enkindled with love for God, a love with no limits. The happiness of all mankind in God, through the Immaculata—behold his dream.

<u>Therefore, he is not indifferent</u> to the spreading evil, but wholeheartedly hates it and hunts down on every occasion, in every place and at every time, all evil that is poisoning the souls of men.

<u>However, he does not trust himself,</u> but mindful that left alone by himself he can do nothing, and that whatever he has and can do he has received from God, and realizing also that the Mediatrix of all graces is the Immaculata, he places boundless hope in Her.

Besides, he clearly understands that conversion, sanctification, perseverance in good, are the work of divine grace. Divine grace is a gift of divine mercy, and in St. Bernard's words, Almighty God entrusted the entire order of grace to His Most Holy Mother, the Immaculata. She is unable to abandon anyone, because never was it heard that anyone who fled to Her was left alone.

Therefore, the simplest way to save a soul is to inspire it to at least do or suffer anything, even the smallest thing, for the gracious Queen, by the will of Almighty God, of heaven and earth.

Therefore, he promotes devotion to Her and filial love for Her with all his zeal.

He is not limited to generalities but diligently looks around himself in order to conquer as many souls as possible for the Immaculata. Provided they do not scorn it, he prudently gives them Her *Knight* to read. [...] Then, he urges them to enroll in the Militia of the Immaculata.

Make them understand that one does not need much time to give oneself forever to the Immaculata, to wear Her medal and repeat once a day the short ejaculatory prayer. Let them but do something for the Immaculata, and slowly She will enter their hearts, purify them, and enkindle in them a joyous love for the Heart of Jesus. And if an acquaintance or relative does not want to think even of the Immaculata, perhaps sew Her medal into his clothes, so that the Immaculata will lovingly pursue him; and pray, fervently pray, that She will deign to win that heart for Herself. A prayer both simple and sublime indicated by the same Immaculata appearing at Lourdes—is the Holy Rosary. May it become the sword of every Knight and Lady of the Immaculata, as Her medal is the bullet that strikes down evil.

Where more members of the Militia of the Immaculata are found, let them from time to time and together arrange how to cleverly, systematically, and energetically lead this holy war to conquer souls for the Immaculata, and thus make them happy.

Above all, the Knight and Lady of the Immaculata remember well that they are instruments in the Immaculata's hands. Therefore, they do not permit sin to be in their hearts even for a moment, but if they unfortunately sometimes fall into it, they erase it at once with an act of perfect contrition, with the resolve to confess at the earliest opportunity. They also remember to at least <u>once per month</u> receive into their hearts God in the Blessed Sacrament of the Altar. And...they fear, <u>very much fear</u>, that they will at any time attribute to themselves even the smallest good that the Immaculata deigns to accomplish through them.

They well know that without Her they will accomplish nothing, yet with Her help <u>nothing will be able to resist them.</u>

※ ※ ※

<u>O Immaculata, Queen of Heaven, be as soon as possible the true QUEEN of Thy whole earth and every individual soul.</u>

Rycerz Niepokalanej

58. Queen of Poland

[Rycerz Niepokalanej, May 1925, pp. 97–102]

It was April 1, 1656.

In the Lwow cathedral, King John Casimir, surrounded by clergy, senators, nobility, and peasants, kneels before the altar of the Blessed Virgin Mary and on behalf of the entire nation takes a vow:

"Great Mother of the God-Man, and Virgin! I, John Casimir, by Thy Son's mercy, the King of Kings and my Lord, and by Thy grace, king, presenting myself at Thy Most Holy feet, make this covenant: I take Thee today as my Patroness and <u>Queen of my dominions</u>. I recommend myself and my Polish Kingdom, the Grand Duchies of Lithuania, Ruthenia, Prussia, Mazovia, Samogitia, Livonia, and Czernihów, and both nations' armies and all the populace, to your particular care and protection. In my kingdom's present tribulation, I humbly beg your help and mercy against the enemies...

"And since, constrained by Thy great kindnesses, I am compelled with the Polish nation to accept a new and fervent obligation to serve Thee, I, in my name as in that of my ministers, senators, nobles, and commoners, promise Thee and Thy Son Jesus Christ, our Savior, that I will spread Thy honor and glory through all the lands of the Polish Kingdom. When by Thy  Son's mercy I will obtain victory over the Swedes, I will do everything to ensure that the anniversary is solemnly celebrated in my state till the end of the world, in remembrance of this grace of God, and Thine, Virgin Most Pure!

"And since with great sorrow of my heart I recognize that the various plagues afflicting my kingdom for seven years bear the just punishment of my God for the groans and oppression of the poor populace of tillers of the soil, oppressed by the soldiers, I bind myself such that after the conquest of peace I will, in union with the republic states, earnestly seek that henceforth the afflicted populace will be free from all oppression. And since Thou, Mother of Mercy, Queen and my Lady, have inspired me to make this vow, do Thou obtain for me the grace of mercy from Thy Son, and assistance in fulfilling what I have promised."

The universal "Amen, Amen, Amen" from all the people sealed this vow.

The papal nuncio, Pietro Vidoni, present for this vow, did not refuse to say aloud the Litany of Loreto, adding at the end, at the request of the king, "<u>Queen of Poland</u>, pray for us."

* * *

After regaining freedom, the Polish bishops turned to the Holy Father with the request to establish on May 3 the feast of Queen of the Polish Crown, to fulfill the vow of the king "that the anniversary be solemnly celebrated in the state until the end of the world." The Holy Father granted this request on October 12, 1923.

So the feast of May 3 is not just a celebration that reminds us of the constitution but is the solemnity of <u>our Queen</u>, who in a special way shows love for Her republic.

[...] Devotees and lovers of the Immaculate Queen! For us, May 3 is <u>Her day</u>, and the entire month of May is <u>Her month</u>, especially dedicated to Her honor. So in what way will we show our love? Will we limit ourselves only to ardent sentiments, affectionate words?

No. It would be too little.

She must be the Queen of Poland, and therefore also the Queen of every heart that beats beneath the Polish sky or away from its longed-for homeland. To conquer <u>for Her</u> the hearts of <u>all and every individual</u>—that is our task, especially in this Her month.

How shall we go about it?

First of all, entrust to Her <u>every</u> matter that we undertake, particularly when it comes to conquering souls for Her.

And then?

Do not neglect <u>any</u> opportunity to spread devotion to and love for Her, and try to bring with us as many souls as possible to the May devotions—attending them either in the churches or somewhere far away from the sanctuaries, in the chapels or by roadside images.

What else?

Impose on ourselves a <u>tiny mortification</u> for this intention, that She may reign in the hearts of all, especially in the hearts of those whose conversion we seek.

We, however, Knights and Ladies of the Immaculata, do not limit ourselves only to our homeland, but rather we do not count the cost in prayer and effort, so that She, the Immaculata, will become, and <u>as quickly as possible</u>, the Queen of the <u>whole</u> world and of every individual soul—the Queen of the Soviets, Germany, Czechoslovakia, Romania, Turkey, Greece, Yugoslavia, Bulgaria, Italy, Hungary, Austria, France, Spain, Portugal, England, etc., etc., so that every heart, without exception, will beat with love for Her, because She will, easily and as soon as possible, unite the hearts of the poor inhabitants of this earth with the burning Heart of God, our Savior.

The love of God is the only source of true and sincere love of neighbor. Then, class struggles will disappear, and mankind will approach, as far as possible on this earth, to happiness, a foretaste of that happiness toward which each of us already naturally tends, i.e., to happiness without limits—in God, in paradise.

Rycerz Niepokalanej

59. To the Most Sacred Heart of Jesus through the Immaculata

[Rycerz Niepokalanej, June 1925, pp. 130–132]

"*The love for the Most Sacred Heart of Jesus, in order that as many souls as possible unite with Him through the Immaculata, is our only incentive*"—we read this in Note 2 of diploma of the Militia of the Immaculata.

Here is the ultimate goal to which our efforts aspire.

We clearly profess it also in the "Act of Consecration to the BVM Immaculate," also printed in the diploma and expressing the essence of the Militia of the Immaculata. Therein we turn to the Immaculata to ask, "If Thou willst, use my whole self, without any reservations, to bring about that which was said of Thee, 'She

Behold the saint most united with My Divine Heart.

shall crush thy head,' and, 'Thou alone hast destroyed all heresies throughout the world,' so that I may become a useful instrument in Thy immaculate and most loving hands, to introduce and increase Thy glory to the maximum in so many straying and indifferent souls, <u>and thus to bring about the greatest extension of the blissful kingdom of the Most Sacred Heart of Jesus</u>."

And why through the Immaculata?

"*For,*" we say next, "*wherever Thou dost enter, there Thou dost obtain the grace of conversion and sanctification.*"

From where does such power come to Her?

"*Since through Thy hands all graces flow upon us from the Most Sweet Heart of Jesus,*" we conclude.

As it is, humanly speaking, the Divine Heart is like the heart of a good father of a family. If any of his children are guilty of some fault, the father must punish them, because justice requires it, and even the love for the child does, so that he would not take his guilt lightly. But the father does not like to cause grief for the child, even though he deserves it, and the father would like to have sufficient reason to not inflict the punishment. To forgive without sufficient reason would embolden the offender. But, he would nevertheless like someone to intercede for him so that justice and affectionate love may be satisfied.

Now, burning with love for us who are guilty, the Divine Heart of Jesus finds such a means worthy of the divine wisdom. He gives us, as mother and protectress, His own dearest and beloved Mother, that being who is beyond the saints and angels in holiness, the one to whom He cannot deny anything, as She is His most worthy and most loved Mother. And He gave Her such a heart that She cannot fail to behold even a single tear on earth, that She cannot fail to look after the salvation and sanctification of every person on earth.

And here we have the bridge that leads us to the Sacred Heart of Jesus. He who falls into sin sinks deeply into bad habits, despises God's graces, no longer looks at the good example of others, does not pay attention to salutary inspirations, and becomes unworthy of further graces. Should he then despair? No, never! Because he has a Mother, given to him by God, who with a tender heart follows his every action, every word, every thought. She does not look at whether he is worthy of the grace of mercy. She is simply the Mother of mercy, and therefore She hastens, even though not invoked, to where the misery in souls is the greatest. Indeed, the more the soul is disfigured by sin, the more God's mercy manifests itself, that mercy whose embodiment—is the Immaculata.

Therefore, we are fighting to hand over to the Immaculata the scepter of power over every soul.

In fact, if She only enters into a soul, though it still be filled with misery, debased by its sins and vices, She will not allow the soul to be lost, but rather she immediately obtains for it the grace of enlightenment of mind and strength of will, so that it might repent and rise again. To Jesus through Mary Immaculate—this is our watchword, highlighted by Msgr. Archbishop Sapieha at the pastoral benediction granted to the Militia and also published in the diploma: "We wholeheartedly bless the members of the Militia of the Immaculata; by fighting under <u>Our Lady's banner</u>, may it help the Church <u>to lead</u> the whole world <u>to the feet of Jesus</u>."

※ ※ ※

Two and a half centuries have passed since the time when the incident shown on the first page of this article occurred.

Our Lord Jesus appearing to St. Margaret Alacoque pointed to him who perhaps was the first to build an altar to the Immaculata in Italy—at Rovigo—and whose spiritual sons from the earliest days of their Order celebrated, proclaimed, and defended the privilege of the Immaculate Conception. He pointed to St. Francis and said, "Behold the saint <u>most</u> united with My Divine Heart."

Yes, he who spreads more veneration and love for the Immaculata, he who gains more souls for Her and through Her for the Sacred Heart of Jesus who loved us even unto death on the cross, such a one also demonstrates the <u>greatest</u> love, because it is an <u>active</u> love for the Most Sacred Heart, and most deeply unites himself with Him.

Rycerz Niepokalanej

60. The Carmelite Scapular

[Rycerz Niepokalanej, July 1925, pp. 162–164]

The 16th day of this month is the feast of Our Lady of Mount Carmel. Sometimes you can hear a lot of doubts concerning the scapular, and therefore it won't be out of place to say a few things here, to make some observations about it.

First of all, what is the origin of the name "scapular"?

It comes from the Latin word *scapula* [...], that is, shoulder, because it means a type of religious garment that the Benedictines, Carmelites, and Dominicans wear in addition to the habit and that covers just the shoulders and hangs more or less on the chest and back.

And what is the origin of the scapular?

The guiding ideals of the different orders did not remain enclosed within the convents' walls, but often also spread to the faithful in the midst of the world. They also, as far as it was possible, desired to put them into practice. Thus arose various congregations and confraternities whose members, being unable to wear a proper religious garment like the monks, at least wore badges that reminded them of it. These badges were similar to that shoulder garment and differed especially in regard to color.

What does a scapular look like?

It is composed of two pieces of woolen cloth connected by strings or straps.

Must the scapular be of wool?

Yes; it cannot be made of cotton, linen, silk, or another material, and it cannot be knitted or embroidered. Otherwise the indulgences are not gained. One is allowed, however, to adorn the wool scapulars with woven images, embroidered or sewn. Also, images can be of some other material or different colors. These ornaments, however, cannot be too large, for the scapular must remain the principal part.

What is needed to gain the indulgences and enjoy the scapular's privileges?

1) Each scapular must be blessed by a priest authorized to do this and imposed by an authorized priest. 2) One who has received the scapular must wear it such that one part rests on the chest while the other, connected to the first with strings or straps over the shoulders, hangs between the shoulder blades.

What should be done if the scapular is lost or worn out?

One must make another, but it is not necessary for a priest to formally impose this one, and even the blessing is not necessary (with the exception of the scapular of the Holy Trinity).

Can you wear several scapulars on one pair of strings?

This is not forbidden, but if among the scapulars is a scapular of the Passion, the string cannot be of any material or color, as with other scapulars, but must be wool and red.

What should be done with a worn-out scapular?

It must be burned.

If a man through negligence or for some other reason does not wear the scapular for a long time, must he request a reimposition?

This is not at all necessary, unless the scapular has been rejected in disbelief or contempt.

Which are the most well-known scapulars?

1) of the Most Holy Trinity, 2) of the Most Sacred Heart of Jesus, 3) of the Passion, 4) the Carmelite, 5) of the Seven Sorrows of the Mother of God, and 6) of the Immaculate Conception.

And the Carmelite scapular, what is its origin?

It was July 16, 1251.

Bl. Simon Stock, sixth superior general of the Carmelites, was beseeching the Most Holy Mother to protect the Order, which was passing at the time through serious difficulties, and he saw in a vision the Blessed Virgin Mary, who gave him a scapular, saying, "Take, my son, this thy order's scapular as a sign of my confraternity, which will be for thee and all Carmel's children a great privilege, and whoever dies wearing this scapular will never suffer eternal fire. It is the sign of salvation, a shield in dangers, and a pledge of the eternal covenant."

Subsequently, the Most Holy Mother appeared to Pope John XXII and promised him that She would free from purgatory on the first Saturday immediately after their death those souls who during their life devoutly wore this scapular.

Although these apparitions are not articles of faith, the numerous conversions accomplished through the scapular serve as eloquent proof of their authenticity.

About these apparitions, the Holy Father Paul V says, "Christians <u>may piously believe</u> in what they say about the help experienced by the souls of the members of the confraternity of the Holy Scapular, i.e., that the Blessed Virgin will aid with constant intercession on their behalf, pious prayers, Her merits, and special protection after death, especially on the sabbath day dedicated by the Church to this Mother of God, the souls of brothers and members who have died in the charity of God and in life wore this holy garment."

A strange thing is that those who have been enrolled in the Carmelite scapular either wear it to death and die happily or, if they do not want to amend their lives, die without the scapular.

※ ※ ※

The scapular, the Rosary, and the Miraculous Medal: here are three things that the Immaculata Herself deigned to offer for the salvation of mankind.

R. N.

61. The Secret of Strength and Power

[Rycerz Niepokalanej, September 1925, pp. 225–227]

Sometimes we hear the complaint, "I want to improve myself, I want to be better, but I <u>can't</u>." In history we read about great leaders and conquerors who nonetheless could not subdue their evil inclinations. Such, for instance, was the celebrated Alexander the Great, who died prematurely as a result of—a licentious life.

Looking around us we see the frightful explicit <u>disappearance of all morality</u>, especially among the youth, and even associations are being formed—truly diabolical—that have crime and debauchery in their program. [...]

The cinema, theater, literature, art, directed in large part by the invisible hand of Freemasonry, instead of spreading education are working feverishly under the resolution of the Freemasons: "We will vanquish the Catholic Church not by reasoning, but by the corruption of morals."

How can we resist this?

In similar circumstances it might seem that such a recognition of one's own weakness as "I cannot improve myself" is a sign of humility. But, in reality, beneath there is a <u>hidden pride</u>.

And in what way?

Well, these people admit in many things that they <u>can</u> do this or that, but they are not able in certain circumstances to subdue this or that fault.

All this proves simply that they rely <u>only</u> on their <u>own strength</u> and think that in that limit of their own power they can do this or that.

But this is an untruth, a <u>lie</u>, because by our own power, with ourselves alone, without divine help, we can do <u>nothing</u> and <u>absolutely</u> nothing. All that we are and whatever we have and can do, we have from Almighty God and receive from Him at every moment of our life, because continuance in existence is nothing other than a continuous receiving of that existence.

Therefore, by ourselves alone we can do nothing except only evil, which is precisely the <u>lack</u> of good, of order, of strength.

If we acknowledge this truth and look to God, from whom we receive all that we have at every moment, we would immediately see that He, God, can still give us more, and as our best Father He desires to give us all that we need. But can Almighty God shower a soul with graces when it attributes to itself that which is a divine gift? If He did, He would confirm it in a false and arrogant opinion. When from His mercy He does not give the abundance of His gifts and...even permits a soul to fall, [He does this] so that the soul will finally realize what it is, in itself, so that it will not rely upon itself but will with full confidence give itself to Him. Falls were for the saints—rungs to perfection. But <u>woe</u> to the soul that will not even accept this final medicine, but remaining in its pride says, "I cannot improve myself"—for God is also just and will demand a strict account of every grace granted to us.

So what should we do?

Give ourselves over totally, with unlimited trust, into the hands of divine mercy, whose personification by God's will is the Immaculata. Trust ourselves in nothing, be fearful of ourselves, and trust Her without limit, and in every occasion of doing evil let us turn to Her as a child to its mother, and we will never fall. The saints claim that anyone who during temptation prays to the Mother of God will surely not sin, and whoever throughout his life has recourse to Her with confidence will surely be saved.

R. N.

62. On the Rosary...

[Rycerz Niepokalanej, October 1925, pp. 257–259]

Ding-dong, ding-dong, come to the Rosary, come to the Rosary—the church bells call, and at dusk their toll runs through the streets, pressing into houses, palaces, basements, attics, looming over the countryside, the forests, seeping into peasant cottages, penetrating ears, minds, and hearts...come to the Rosary, come to the Rosary.

Many joyfully expect this signal, and as soon as they hear the first bell toll, they hasten to finish their work, gather together, and go to—the Queen.

But there are others who hesitate. I have so much to do! I'm so tired! I need to rest. Anyway, the Rosary isn't Holy Mass on Sundays and holy days, which one must hear under pain of sin. I have guests. I have arrived from afar. I have to get here or there...a thousand excuses run through their head.

To go or not to go?!

Will not the Mother of God, Queen not only of heaven but also of earth, be able to bless me in my work, so that I perform it more easily, more quickly, and better?... Cannot She arrange circumstances in such a way that they are more favorable for my soul, and even my earthly existence (provided this is not opposed to the more important matter of salvation)?... After all, She wishes better for me than I do for myself, and She can help me, for the Creator would not refuse Her anything. Isn't it better, therefore, to entrust to Her my worries and troubles? She will remedy them, more quickly and more easily than I would.

Tired after working... Yet where can I find more rest and peace than at the foot of Her who is our Mother, our Help, our Refuge, our Comforter?

It is true that one is not under pain of sin in regard to praying the Rosary—but what kind of love would ours be if it were limited to our strict obligations, neglect of which would be a serious transgression? Such conduct would appear more as the service of a slave than the love of child toward his best Father in heaven and most affectionate Mother. No! This is unworthy of a lover of Mary. Such a person seeks rather the opportunity to go to Her as often as possible, to remain at Her feet as long as possible (as long as the duties of one's state allow it). He entrusts to Her all his troubles and worries and his whole life. He reflects and works on how to best make Her work proceed. Her reign in the souls of all those who are and will be, whether these are acquaintances or strangers, friends or foes, relatives, fellow citizens, fellow countrymen and foreigners, Catholics and non-Catholics: this is his aspiration, his wish; here is the goal of his efforts. And where can he draw the light to know what to do and how to act if not at Her feet? Where else can he gain strength for such sublime work?

I have guests at home… So let us go together. Indeed, I also wish them happiness, and our own matters can often be dealt with at another time.

But there are also those who do not go to the Rosary. If their duties of state truly do not permit them, because they must fulfill them precisely at these hours and not at any other time, the Immaculata will accept their ardent wish to go to the common Rosary; She Herself will descend to them and fill their hearts with Her blessing. And those whose love of neighbor compels them to stay by the side of the sick to bring them aid, they need not be sad, they need not worry. The Immaculata will accept their services rendered to the sick.

But what is there to say about those who could go to the Rosary but do not, whether out of laziness or neglect, or sometimes on account of a sinful enjoyment? Can perhaps the Immaculata bless them?

* * *

Ding-dong, ding-dong, come to the Rosary, come to the Rosary, the bells call for the last time. The church is filled already. A painting of the Immaculata glistens on the altar amidst lights. The bell by the sacristy is struck. The service has begun.

"Our Father…" "Hail Mary… Hail Mary…"

A soothing balsam descends upon aching hearts, a ray of hope dawns again in desperate souls. The poor, the weary, those who bend under the burden of worries, troubles, and crosses feel more clearly and explicitly that they are not orphans, that they have a mother, after all, who knows their pains, who sympathizes, who consoles and helps them. They feel that they still have to suffer a little longer, yet a reward will follow—an eternal, infinite reward. It is worthwhile to suffer in this brief life in order to expiate faults committed and to give proof of their love for God. They understand that by suffering the soul is purified as gold in the fire, is detached from the transient delusions that the world calls happiness, and rises higher, infinitely higher, to the Source of all happiness—God. They see that their soul can rest only in Him, and everything else—is too little…

"Lamb of God, who takes away the sins of the world…"

"Under Your protection…" resounds in the church. It is a song that comes from the heart, binding the children's hearts to their Mother's heart.

✳ ✳ ✳

The service is over, the lights go out, and the participants with a blissful peace in their heart, their spirits fortified, return happily to their houses.

R. N.

Recitation of the Rosary at Niepokalanów

63. More Thinking!

[Rycerz Niepokalanej, November 1925, pp. 289–291]

Sometime during this year or the past year, in a railroad car I met quite an intelligent Jew. As a member of the Militia of the Immaculata I consider it my duty to indicate the light of truth also to non-Catholics, and thus I struck up a conversation with him. What do you do? What is the purpose of life? That was our theme. Evidently, we came also to the question, And what will happen after death?

—They will put you into the grave.

—And nothing more? - I ask.

—I do not know - he answers.

—And who should know for you?

—If you please, I have no time to think about it; I am a merchant, and I have so many things to take care of that I cannot give much thought to it.

—And is that wise? Imagine a person who goes on the train here with us and to the question "Where are you going?" seriously responds, "I don't know, I have no time to think about it." Would such a person be sensible?

However, there is no need to look to non-Christians, because among Catholics how many are those who, although they attend Holy Mass on Sundays and holy days, do not neglect holy confession, and avoid major transgressions, rarely, very rarely, give some deep thought to this—which is exactly the ultimate purpose of life. Rarely will they say to themselves, "I, <u>indeed</u> also <u>I</u>—will die. <u>I</u> will render an account to God for every day of my life, for every action, word, and even <u>thought</u>. Now <u>I</u> have time to gain merit and this <u>present time only</u>, because from the moment when I breathe my last breath I will <u>never</u> have such a favorable time as the present. From this world I will take nothing, <u>absolutely nothing</u>; I cannot bring anything with me to the next world. What <u>stupidity</u>, then, it is to chase after that which passes, to seek momentary happiness, which quickly vanishes, at the expense of eternity."

From time to time, however, these and similar thoughts must find a place amidst the tumult of worries and troubles. The month of November, All Souls' Day, prayers for the departed, visits to the cemetery—these are occasions for such thoughts, which are serious and of primary importance.

It is true that the mind turns away from eternal truth when the heart is stained with sin. Then one would prefer not to think about it, or even to say to oneself, "Let us leave alone life after death, they will put you into the grave and that's it." No one, after all, has yet come back from the other world.

Someone has gone somewhere else and hasn't come back, and therefore doesn't exist?—what logic! But even though this is so illogical, the excuse fails when confronted by the facts, because indeed many from the next world explicitly gave knowledge about themselves. Suffice it to mention the recently canonized St. Thérèse of the Child Jesus, who generously keeps her promise and sends down a true "shower of roses" of spiritual and material assistance throughout the world. It is enough to look closely in the Museum of the Poor Souls in Purgatory (in Rome at Trastevere) and to see the numerous imprints left by souls from purgatory that appeared, asking for prayers.

But a heart corrupted by sin fears eternity, thus it avoids thinking of it.

What can one do about it?

Not thinking about it does not lessen the reality, so one <u>must</u> think about it. However, we have now a Mother in heaven, the personification of divine mercy, the Immaculata. So if the thought of your past life and sins oppresses you, if you do not dare to look into the future beyond the grave, give yourself to Her totally, without limit; entrust to Her the matter of your entire salvation, your whole life, death, and eternity; confess your sins sincerely and trust Her fully, and you will know what peace and happiness is, a foretaste of heaven, and you will sigh for heaven.

If you have never experienced this, try it out, see whether it is true, and you will find out.

R. N.

64. From the Publisher

[Rycerz Niepokalanej, December 1925, front cover]

This issue closes the fourth publishing year of *Knight of the Immaculata*. How many souls has the Immaculata drawn through it to Herself, how many souls has She given peace and happiness—we do not know. However, we have received quite a few letters in which the writers with the greatest gratitude have given thanks for the *Knight*, declaring that henceforth they desire to give themselves totally to the Immaculata, to ignite love everywhere and to arouse confidence in Her and spread Her *Knight*, and simultaneously they confessed that they have become convinced that any happiness other than God is impossible. <u>Glory to Her forever.</u>

How much evil there still is in our homeland!!... Can we look upon this with indifference? Evil is spreading, infecting the cities and villages and poisoning especially the youth.

Who will remedy this?

The Immaculata.

Let Her only reach out to souls lacking virtue, let Her take possession of hearts, and the face of the earth will be transformed. [...]

65. The Latest Fashion

[Kalendarz Rycerza Niepokalanej, 1926, p. 84]

"We will not conquer the Church by reasoning, but by the corruption of morals"—the Masons adopted this at a convention. And they began to sow immorality through theaters, cinema, books, magazines, paintings, sculptures, etc., and ever more through—pardon the expression—pig's fashion. How many souls perish by this!!!...

But let them keep in mind [the wearing of] "the latest fashion..." in the coffin, let them take refuge in the Immaculata, and they will become sober.

The present Holy Father, Pope Pius XI, has himself composed the following prayer to the Immaculata concerning modesty in dress and enriched it with an indulgence of 300 days:

"Mary, Immaculate Virgin, as Holy Church expresses, cover us with the mantle of Your holiness, so that we may clothe ourselves in the holy purity of morals, resisting the scandal, coming above all from reprehensible fashion in dress, from reading bad books and perverse newspapers. Obtain for us that we may give a good example, especially in our dealings with our neighbor, in our dress, and in our choice of books and magazines for reading, so that in this regard we do not give scandal. We offer You these our firm resolutions, so that You may present them to Your divine Son, in order to ask pardon and to make amends to Him for these scandals, which we see at the present time, often even among Catholics, and which are an offense to the divine Majesty. Amen."

66. Penance, Penance, Penance...

[Rycerz Niepokalanej, February 1926, pp. 33–35]

Indulge yourself and be merry—the world cries out. In pursuit of ever more pleasure one may commit theft, fraud, treachery, corrupt oneself, and even murder. And when a man cannot get any more pleasure or when his heart is filled with moral filth, he experiences all the emptiness and triviality of this deceptive happiness that he pursued, and if he lacks humility, which draws one toward the way of penance, toward God, life becomes ugly and sometimes ends with vile suicide.

* * *

On the 11th of this month we celebrate the anniversary, acclaimed throughout the world, of the Immaculata's apparition in Lourdes.

What did She recommend to us?

Here is what the fortunate chosen one of the Immaculata, Bernadette, tells her parish priest, who had asked the Lady that was appearing to her to make a rose bush bloom in winter, as a sign that She was from heaven.

"I have seen," she says, "the Wonderful Creature and said to Her, 'The parish priest requires some sort of proof, for example, that you, My Lady, make the rose bush bloom that is under your feet, because my word is not sufficient for the priests, and they do not want me to speak about it (about the building of a chapel).' When I said this, She smiled but said not a word; then She told me to pray for sinners and said three times,

'Penance! penance! penance!'"

To make a rose bush bloom in the winter is a trifle, even if wrought by the Immaculata, compared to the conversion of sinners by means of—penance.

* * *

In this month Holy Church invites us in a special way to practice penance, sprinkling ashes on our heads and saying, "Remember, man, thou art dust and unto dust thou shalt return." And on February 17 the Church commands the commencement of the fast.

[...] [Thus Catholics can] do penance for their sins and for the many insults offered to God throughout the world.

R. N.

Article in the 1938 *Kalendarz Rycerza Niepokalanej* (Calendar of the Knight of the Immaculata) on Our Lady of Fatima, who had again requested penance

67. Heaven

[Rycerz Niepokalanej, February 1926, pp. 36–38]

On December 16 of last year, I had just got on a railway carriage and with some effort was loading a large package. The rattle of irons betrayed its contents.

—Those are bookbinding blades - said a Jewish man sitting in front of me with a beard that had turned gray.

—That's right - I confirmed.

—I know, because I have three large binding machines; however, nowadays there is not work as there was before.

—I am taking these blades to have them sharpened; where do you have yours sharpened? - I asked.

He offered the name of a firm and showed a willingness to talk longer, so I asked him right away,

—Excuse me, could I ask you what your purpose in life is?

—Purpose?

—Yes, what is it that you aspire to? What do you ultimately wish to accomplish?

—To be honest, to do wrong to no one, so that people may say, "That is an honest man."

—Isn't that too little?

—Too little? A good reputation is a lot.

—But if by living as you said we yet meet with ingratitude (which often happens), what then? Would it still be worthwhile to be honest?

—True, it is not enough.

—But, don't you envision anything else after death? - interjected an intellectual sitting beside us (later we found out that he was a lawyer).

—What do we know about that? They bury a man under the ground, and there he will be all right; you do not need to eat, or drink, or pay rent. Oh, if we could live without eating, it would be good to live in the world.

—I just wish to die as soon as possible - spoke still another, a young Jewish man. - What kind of life is this, when there is no purpose. It would be fine if people did not love money. Among us, it is written in Holy Scripture that the rabbi is to be a man who does not love money.

—Perhaps in the Talmud - I corrected.

—In the Talmud - he repeated - because only then can one rightly judge, yet still the rabbis are attached to money. The best thing would be to leave for the next world as soon as possible.

—What is there in the next world; everything ends here - interjected the old man.

—You gentlemen are of the same religious beliefs, it is probable you agree on this point - I said.

—Among us this is not taught clearly - the young man added.

—You have studied this - the old man says to me - tell us what you think.

—Yes, of course: let us look only within ourselves. Do we want to live a long life?

—Not me, because the more you live the more you have to suffer.

—But if we were doing well and every good thing were in great abundance?

—But it is not like that in the world.

—But if it were?

His sad eyes brightened up.

—If this were true, then yes.

—And for how long? Would you not wish to live as long as possible?

—Obviously I would.

—So we wish to live, but without suffering, and in not just any happiness, but we would prefer that it be great rather than little, and even the consideration itself of any insurmountable limit in this happiness would be for us an obstacle to this happiness; we desire happiness, but without limits.

—Indeed.

—Not only that, but we want this happiness to last a long time, as long as possible...forever.

—Quite so.

—Evidently such a happiness without limits cannot be found in this limited world; it can be found only in the infinite, eternal God: in heaven.

And subsequently all of us here present desire this, and every person, regardless of differences in nationality, lives in this desire. It comes from something common to us all, namely, from our human nature. Could God, who has bestowed on man abilities and natural desires to reach his goal—eyes, to see visible objects, and such objects that really exist; ears, to hear sounds, and such sounds that really exist—could God give man a higher intellectual longing and not give him the means to satisfy it?

Such a longing would then be purposeless. If God created in our nature this somehow unquenchable desire for happiness with the explicit intention that it have no limits and did not provide the means to satisfy this burning thirst, He would not be acting reasonably or with kindness—in short, He would not be God. Therefore, there must be such happiness.

This is confirmed—in spite of the reasoning of all kinds of know-it-alls, big and small—by the many apparitions of those who have left this world and now are enjoying eternal happiness and rightfully wish to help us here on earth.

In recent times, a true "shower of roses" of all kinds of graces has been sent down by the recently departed, and already canonized, St. Thérèse of the Child Jesus, whose own sister is now the superior of the Carmelite Sisters in Lisieux.

This is our common goal.

M. K.

68. Miracles

[Rycerz Niepokalanej, March 1926, pp. 68–70]

Not long ago I spoke with "One" and "Other"; I am not giving names because perhaps they would not want that. We talked about truths, theses, hypotheses, etc., and we also touched on miracles.

"One" declared with a tone of outrage that some bishop had believed too hastily in a miracle and had sent a priest to the place to investigate the matter.

—If he believed right away, then why has he sent the priest to investigate - I asked.

—...I'm just repeating what the newspaper said.

—Well then, how wisely they write about this, wouldn't you say? As regards events that are considered to be miraculous, the Church proceeds very cautiously and sends to the place a commission composed of laity and expert clergy in order to establish the facts, circumstances, and characteristics before it decides on whether or not the occurrence is truly miraculous.

—We quite often encounter miracles - interjected "Other" - because we still do not know so many laws of nature.

—How exactly do you envisage the concept of a miracle, sir? - I said.

—It is an occurrence originating in forces of nature still unknown to us.

—That is certainly not a miracle.

—Then what is?

It is an occurrence <u>not</u> originating <u>in forces of nature</u> known or unknown but immediately caused by God's omnipotence, contrary to the existing laws of nature. Given our finite head, we would like to narrow everything into its notions. So as we always see in daily life natural causes in different instances, we are inclined to include all events in this category, at most, with this difference, that in some— we still do not know the causes. But the universe is greater, one may say almost infinitely greater, than all our heads put together, and everything does not necessarily have to come from natural causes, that is to say, material causes. Almighty God, who created everything out of nothing, all that surrounds us, who maintains us in existence, is giving existence to everything at every moment, and He is not so weak that He cannot do things that transcend His creatures or that do not strictly obey their given laws.

Indeed, this immediate action of God greatly contributes to reviving faith and stirring up increased confidence in God. This is true in regard to ordinary things, but we get so accustomed even to God's greatest works that they no longer make an impression on us. Thus, this immediate action of God is from time to time necessary for our good.

—I do not deny that Almighty God can perform miracles, but I would like to hear the facts.

—Yes, of course. I personally know a very well-educated and holy priest who told me these facts about himself:

"When I was a little boy, my foot ached in such a way that I could not sleep and would scream with pain at night. The doctors were unable to help, and finally they held a consultation and decided that an operation was necessary.

"It was evening; the next day they were supposed to perform the operation. My mother, however, seeing what was going on, removed all the bandages and poured water from Lourdes on the aching foot. This was the first night in which I slept. In the morning I arose—completely well. The doctors came for the operation, and I was already walking freely. They were stupefied. But it does not end at this; as if to demonstrate that it was not a mere trifle, I still could not put on my shoes because of a bulge on my foot, which later opened up, and a piece of bone came out of it. The doctor who treated me was an unbeliever; but after this incident, he was converted and had a church built."

Or the cure of Peter Rudder, known throughout the world:

During the cutting down of trees, a tree fell on his leg and broke it so badly that despite medical treatments the bones not only did not coalesce but even began to fester. He was bedridden amidst awful pain for a whole year, and then for eight years and two months he dragged himself about on crutches. But having devotion to the Blessed Virgin since childhood, he went to Oostacker, where a grotto had been constructed similar to the grotto at Lourdes and where the Immaculata was venerated. The parts of the broken bones stuck out about three centimeters apart, the lower part of the leg was swinging inertly in all directions, and coming out of the wound was so foul-smelling a substance that the driver exclaimed, "Here is a man who is losing his leg on the way," and the train conductor reproached him, saying that he was polluting the carriage. Having come to the grotto he began to pray. Suddenly he stood up completely well. His doctor, Mr. Affenaer, before an unbeliever, was converted and became a fervent Catholic.

These are miracles.

M. K.

69. When Will It Come to Pass?...

[Rycerz Niepokalanej, May 1926, pp. 130–131]

Bl. Catherine Labouré, the privileged nun to whom the Immaculata deigned to appear in Paris, in the chapel of the Motherhouse of the Sisters of Charity, and whom She used as an instrument in the introduction and propagation of the Miraculous Medal, prophetically foreseeing the day when the Immaculata will receive honor from all, exclaimed, "Oh how nice, how nice it will be to hear, 'Mary is <u>Queen of the whole world</u>.' And all Her children will repeat, 'She is the <u>Queen of each one of us</u>.'"

How can we hasten this moment?...we, the Knights and Ladies of the Immaculata, who for this ideal have totally consecrated ourselves to the Immaculata?...

The month of May has dawned again, Her month, our Queen, Lady and dearest Mother.

She looks upon the whole world, seeing each person in the secrets of his heart, and She knows the thoughts and desires of each one of us.

She looks into our hearts to find any manifestation of love, any movement of fervor, even the smallest, so that She may lavish us with graces and take us to Herself after death.

And in this Her month, could we not do something special for Her?...

But what should we do?

1) If the duties of our state permit, we should not neglect to attend the May devotions. Let us not merely go alone but also bring with us our relatives and friends, especially those who shun the church.

2) We should promote the Militia of the Immaculata with greater zeal, that in Her month the number of Her Knights and Ladies may increase greatly.

3) Let us distribute Her medal, wherever possible and to children, so that they will always wear it around their necks, and to the elderly, and to the youth in particular, so that under Her protection they will have enough strength to resist the manifold temptations and pitfalls lying in wait for them in our times. And also to those who do not go to church, who are afraid to go to confession, who mock religious practices, who laugh at the truths of the Faith, who are mired in a moral swamp or are living in heresy outside the Church—oh! to these it is absolutely indispensable to offer the Immaculata's medal, and ask them to wear it, and at the same time fervently beg the Immaculata for their conversion. Many manage to accomplish this, even when someone does not want in any way to accept the medal. They just sew it secretly into his or her clothing and pray for that person, and sooner or later the Immaculata will show what She can do. The Miraculous Medal therefore is the bullet of the Militia of the Immaculata.

4) And...let Her *Knight* in this month gain more and more souls for the Immaculata. [...] and read the *Knight of the Immaculata*.

※ ※ ※

When, O Immaculata, will that blessed hour come, in which every heart on earth will love Thee sincerely and, loving Thee, burn with love for the Sacred Heart of God our Savior?...

R. N.

70. Our Power

[Rycerz Niepokalanej, October 1926, pp. 289–291]

In the *Protocols of the Elders of Zion*, i.e., of the true leadership of Freemasonry, they write about themselves: "Who or what is capable of overthrowing an invisible power? And this is precisely what our power is. External Freemasonry serves to conceal its objectives, while this power's plan of action, and even the place where it is located, will never be known to the people."

Gentlemen, fortunately for you, we are capable of overthrowing even an invisible power! I say "fortunately for you" because you have no idea how sweet it is to faithfully serve God and the Immaculata.

I maintain that we are capable of overthrowing you, and we shall overthrow you.

Perhaps you are curious about who we are, that we trust in our own power. Well we are an army, whose Commander knows every one of you, who has observed and observes every one of your deeds, hears every one of your words, and even...even none of your thoughts escapes His attention. Tell us yourselves whether under these circumstances there can be talk of secret plans, of concealment and invisibility?

Worse yet (actually better yet for you), you are so checkmated that you can only make those moves that our Commander allows for His wise purposes, and you would have long ago been crushed to dust if our Commander had only nodded His consent, and to Him alone are you indebted that the earth still suffers you to live upon its surface—how merciful toward you He is.

And do you know why?

Because our Commander loves you. Could you ever imagine that? He loves you very much and does not desire your perdition, but He delays and waits for you to reflect on your life and... as quickly as possible join His ranks. But the time will come, and soon, for every one of you, when it will be too late!!!...

Do you know what our Commander's name is?

It is Immaculata, Refuge of Sinners, but also Vanquisher of the Infernal Serpent.

Tell us where you can go to escape from Her gaze? What deed, word, or plan do you think you can somehow conceal from Her?

You are dust of the earth!—do you not receive your existence together with your treasures at every moment from God's hand? Is not He, the Just One, able to annihilate you into dust?

But behold, our Commander, the Immaculata, prays for mercy for you, for a prolongation of your life, so that you can still come to your senses.

But soon the moment will come, and you will close your eyes forever, and if now in life you do not regularize your relationship with God, it will be a terrible moment! Then regrets, tears, and penance will be of no avail! Consider all of this, calmly and seriously— and...do what your conscience will indicate to you...

✳ ✳ ✳

Knights and Ladies of the Immaculata and all of you who read these words, in this month of the Rosary, October, seek as diligently as possible to attend the common Rosary, whether in churches or along the roads, whether near paintings or statues of Our Lady. Whoever cannot leave home, let him at home recite a third part [five decades] of the Rosary daily.

And why?

Because the Immaculata Herself deigned to urge us to pray the Holy Rosary, appearing to Bl. Bernadette with rosary in hand.

And for whom?

For whom would it be more than precisely these our poor unfortunate brothers, the Masons, the more unfortunate in that they do not see that they rush toward their own perdition, and yet they are our brothers. For after all, Our Lord Jesus did not exclude them from participation in the merits of His Passion.

And for what intention?

Would you not think it best, Dear Readers, that they convert as quickly as possible, even join the Militia of the Immaculata? And that, desirous to repair the evils hitherto perpetrated, they zealously, following the example of St. Paul after his conversion, take it upon themselves to work for the salvation of souls?...

R. N.

71. HELL

[Rycerz Niepokalanej, October 1926, pp. 291–292]

—It is impossible that Almighty God punishes souls in hell.

—And why is that?

—Because, after all, Almighty God is merciful, infinitely merciful; therefore, how could He so severely punish?

—But He is also just and that infinitely; therefore, He cannot pass over any guilt not yet blotted out, nor any punishment not thoroughly satisfied.

—Is there not enough suffering already in this world?

—Those who suffer are usually the good and the gentle, and precisely those who steal, exploit, and cheat others often indulge themselves and live as they please. Therefore, in this world there is still no balancing of accounts.

—Well, I understand, but does it have to be eternity in hell!

—The offense is measured by the dignity of the one offended. A slap across the cheek directed against a street sweeper is an offense, but a slap given to the mayor of the city would be a greater offense, and against the president of the Republic an even greater one; and the offense to an infinitely higher Being, God, is infinitely greater. Therefore, the satisfaction must also be infinitely greater. Through the sacrament of holy confession the infinite merits of the Passion of Our Lord Jesus strictly and fully atone for this offense. He who does not wish to avail himself of the precious Blood of the God-Man will not be capable, as a finite creature, to give infinite satisfaction in this life: therefore, he will have to be compelled to do it after death by suffering infinitely, that is, eternally. Reason requires this.

R. N.

72. Why?...

[Rycerz Niepokalanej, January 1929, p. 5]

Why do many people today try to talk themselves and others into the idea that there is no God, though they know perfectly well that all the learned men cannot even put together the necessary elements to create a measly mosquito? And to maintain that supposedly everything came to be by some inexplicable accident is absurd—the same as if one thought that one's wristwatch by itself, without anybody's help, for no particular reason, by accident...was formed!

Why do so many otherwise intelligent and educated people in various fields not seek to recognize completely their life's purpose and their relationship with God? Why are they in other matters usually advanced, but in the most important question so very backward?

Why is it that so many are able to find the appropriate books to obtain knowledge, but about the Catholic religion they learn from inadequate, often murky sources, rather than take in hand the most reliable and clear book—the catechism?

Why is all this?

M.

73. Our War

[Rycerz Niepokalanej, March, 1932, pp. 133–134]

Looking around and seeing so much evil everywhere, we honestly would like, especially as members of the Militia of the Immaculata, to redress this evil, to bring people to the Most Sacred Heart of Jesus through the Immaculata and thus make our brothers all over the world eternally happy, and even already on this earth: hence a war against evil, an implacable, constant, victorious—war.

But in what does it consist? Where do we find its first, most important nucleus? Where should we strike first?

Sometimes it seems to us that Almighty God does not govern this world "energetically enough." After all, He could with one movement of His almighty will crush and grind into dust people like [the Mexican President Plutarco] Calles, the atheists in the Soviet Union, the Spanish church-burners, and the immoral poisoners of youth. Thus thinks our finite, narrow head, whereas the Eternal Wisdom judges otherwise. Persecution purifies the soul like fire, the executioners' hands create multitudes of martyrs, and the persecutors sometimes experience in the end the grace of conversion. Inscrutable and always most wise are God's ways.

It does not follow that we are to cross our arms and let the enemy of human souls romp freely. Not at all. But...

But…let us not desire to correct Infinite Wisdom, to guide the Holy Ghost, but rather we must let Him guide us.

Let us imagine that we are a paintbrush in the hand of an infinitely perfect painter. What must the brush do in order that the most beautiful painting can be created? It must allow itself to be guided as perfectly as possible. The brush might still have pretensions to correcting an earthly, finite, fallible painter, but when the Eternal Wisdom, God, uses us as instruments, we will act in the most perfect way when we allow ourselves to be guided most perfectly and completely.

We gave ourselves, through the act of consecration, to the Immaculata as Her complete property. She is undoubtedly the most perfect instrument in God's hands, and we should be instruments in Her immaculate hands.

So when will we combat most rapidly and most perfectly the evil throughout the world? When we let ourselves be most perfectly guided by Her. And this is the only and most important matter.

I said—the only one. Truly, each of us must seek nothing other than agreement, conformity, complete merging, as it were, of our will with Her will, just as Her will is totally united to God's will, Her heart with the heart of Her Son, Jesus.

This matter—is the only one. Whatever we do, even if it is more than heroic and shakes the foundation of all evil on earth, it will only have value if in doing it our will agrees with Her will, and through Her with God's will. Therefore, there is only one thing, i.e., the fusion of our will with Her will, that has some value and—the entire value. This is the essence of love (not feelings, although these also can be beautiful), which will change us through the Immaculata into God, which will inflame us and through us set the world on fire and destroy, consume in it, all evil. This is the fire of which the Savior said, "I came to cast fire on the earth: what will I, but that it be kindled?" (Lk 12:49).

Having set ourselves aflame by this fire of divine love (I repeat, it does not consist in sweet tears and feelings but comes from the will, even in the midst of aversion and repugnance), we will inflame the whole world.

But we must set ourselves on fire, we must not let ourselves cool down, but rather we must burn more and more strongly; we must melt ourselves and become one with God through the Immaculata.

We must, therefore, concentrate all our attention on this and only on this: to unite ourselves closely with the hand of our Lady, our Leader, that She might do with us what She pleases.

And this is the essential condition for the MI: "give oneself totally to the Immaculata as an instrument in Her immaculate hands."

Then and only then will we conquer souls for the Immaculata, and through Her we will be united to the fire of love of the Most Sacred Heart of Jesus, and we will melt the whole world and every individual soul.

I write from the land of Japan, on the day of the apparition of the Immaculata at Lourdes.

M. K.

74. THE MONTH OF MAY

[Mugenzai no Seibo no Kishi, May 1932, pp. 98–99]

The winter wind has now stopped, the snow and ice have melted, the fields have become verdant, the sun shines pleasantly—inexpressibly pleasing sentiments are awakened in this month of May, which has just arrived.

It has come, and it is pleasing to us, this month of May, in which the soul is filled with beauty greater even than that which is found in nature. The altars of Mary throughout the Catholic Church, with beautifully adorned statues or paintings of Her, strongly attract the hearts of many. The faithful, after completing their daily work, gather in the evening, in the church, and open their hearts to Mary. They thank Her for the graces they receive incessantly from God through Her intercession. They entrust to Her their worries, troubles, and difficulties and ask for deliverance from them and for Her protection.

The souls shackled with the bonds of sin and immersed in evil sincerely repent of their sins, arise from former chains, and abandon evil, as newly blooming plants return to a new radiant life, and these souls ask for mercy, patience, and strength for a new journey.

Dear Readers! If anyone among you does not understand the words above or has doubts about them, in the evening let him out of necessity look for a Catholic church and listen to what is said about Mary the Mother of Jesus. He will experience what the numerous children gathered there have, and he will understand well what I say.

Korube

75. VISIT OF MRS. KAWAI, THE WIFE OF THE MINISTER PLENIPOTENTIARY, IN NIEPOKALANÓW [1]

[Mugenzai no Seibo no Kishi, December 1933, pp. 371–373]

Before my return to Japan—August 27, at about three o'clock in the afternoon—Mrs. Kawai with her family visited Niepokalanów. She came with her two daughters, Cecilia [2] and Genevieve, as well as her mother, Mrs. Narahara, and two servants [3]. As soon as they got out of the taxi they entered the church to visit the Blessed Sacrament. According to the monastery's rules, women may not go inside—so we arranged a reception in the parlor. On that day, the parlor was adorned with the flags of both countries, Poland and Japan. Particularly conspicuous were the numerous flowers at the feet of the statue of the Immaculata, and on the walls were hung numerous photographs of the life and work of the monks in Niepokalanów. We showed these to the guests, and among them were photographs of the Japanese Niepokalanów, and these aroused particular interest.

Soon a record player was set up, and a few Japanese discs were played. And after the modest reception at the monastery, we led the guests to a nearby hill area, where we informed them about the clearly visible areas of the monastery buildings. We used this method because of the fact that women, as aforementioned, are not allowed to enter the monastery.

The guests, at six in the evening, graciously said good-bye and departed.

Korube

[1] In the [original] text are three photographs with the following captions: 1) The family of the deceased envoy, Kawai, in front of the entrance to the monastery. 2) In front, Mrs. Kawai, the wife of the minister plenipotentiary, and her mother Mrs. Narahara; behind, Mrs. Kubo and Mrs. Rose Takahashi. 3) The family bids me farewell at the station in Warsaw. - editor of the *Pisma*.
[2] Maria Cecilia. - editor of the *Pisma*.
[3] Mrs. Sue Kubo and Rose Takahashi. - editor of the *Pisma*.

76. Knowledge

[Rycerz Niepokalanej, April 1934, p. 101]

What follows did not occur in Japan.

In a railroad car I met a gentleman who greatly praised human knowledge, and it appeared that he was ready to decide on any problem in life. I asked him which branch of knowledge is so certain of itself. He replied, "Medicine." I had to present to him that it is admitted that medicine is still largely groping along.

✳ ✳ ✳

But even more, one can find people who almost deify today's knowledge, as in the past, in antiquity, the sun, stones, trees, animals, etc. were deified in various countries.

It is true that science today has found answers to a number of questions, but we cannot deceive ourselves, for in one hundred, or perhaps fifty, years, the people of that time will look back upon the findings of today with a certain pitifulness, just as we look upon the knowledge acquired decades ago. And perhaps they will accuse us for not having sufficiently used what we had at our disposition and not having gained all that we could have acquired, or perhaps should have acquired.

In any case, whenever we are comparing the number of solved questions to those for which we have only unclear answers or have not yet found answers, we must admit that all the so-loudly praised knowledge of today is only a small babe in the cradle. Rightly, a professor at a university in Rome, Goretti, a Jesuit, stated that by studying natural phenomena we come at most to the fourth or fifth "why," and then we can no longer find an answer. For example: My pen dropped. Why did it drop? Because the earth attracted it. And why did the earth attract it?... Why do objects attract each other? And here we can no longer give a definite answer. We have only different suppositions. So already at the second "why" we get stuck.

When will we reach the hundredth, thousandth, and so on "why"? So knowledge is really only in its infancy.

※ ※ ※

I would not discourage anyone from obtaining knowledge, of course; he who has the opportunity to do so, let him study and research as much as possible, but I would like to draw attention to two things:

First, we must not overestimate human knowledge and must be able to humbly confess that many, very many, mysteries are and will be obscure to us. And as far as mysteries containing in themselves the concept of the infinite, as that of God, the divine life, etc., we will never be able with our finite reason to fathom them.

Second, it would be irrational for a person to submerge himself in the study of the atom or another detail of knowledge to the point of forgetting about the ultimate purpose of his life and the means leading thereto, and to only on his deathbed ponder whether there is life after death or not.

M. K.

77. Memories of the Past Four Years

[Mugenzai no Seibo no Kishi, May 1934, pp. 130–131]

[...] Four years ago, on April 24, when on the ship *Nagasaki* I arrived with two brothers to the port of Nagasaki, I asked myself, How will they receive me in Japan? When I arrived by taxi at the church in Oura (which is now declared a national monument), a large white statue of Our Lady with the inscription "Our Lady of Japan" at the base seemed to be inviting me to enter the church. I was worn out with seasickness, but when I saw the statue, the weariness went away and I joyfully entered the church.

For a week after my arrival, I lived near the church in Oura and often looked at the white statue of Our Lady of Japan. [...]

Korube

78. How We Come to Know God

[Rycerz Niepokalanej, August 1934, p. 228]

Every day we come to know many new things; we all understand this well from everyday experience.

How do we come to know about things?

When I see a beautiful painting, it comes to my mind that the painter must be gifted, and I begin to feel a reverence for that man, because I have come to know him as the creator of the painting. But that is a very imperfect knowledge of that gifted man. When I ask, however, who this painter is and someone who knows him personally tells me about him, I will come to know him much more, relying on the words of this man's testimony. When I finally meet that man, see him, talk to him, I will by now know him incomparably better than before.

This is our way of acquiring knowledge. The simplest and clearest is by direct encounter with the object of knowledge. Less perfect is indirectly, through the testimony of others who have encountered the object. And this knowledge is based on faith in the one who testifies to us. Even less clearly is from the effects. This knowledge is based on reasoning, that is, knowledge of a cause from its effects.

There are relatively few things with which we have the opportunity to directly come into contact. We live in such a fraction of time and space that everything that has happened up until the moment of our coming into the world, and that which we do not perceive because it is far away from our current location, eludes irretrievably this first way of attaining knowledge; even our cognitive faculties have rather well-defined limits. Therefore, there are very few things we directly encounter.

A much greater scope for attaining knowledge is the second way, i.e., by faith in others. Schools, libraries, books, newspapers, radio—all these provide us with things to be believed. And the most fervent rationalist from morning till night makes countless acts of faith in what he learns from others.

The extent of attaining knowledge through the causes from the effects is also very great. All education and a large portion of daily life are based on this knowledge.

It is not otherwise with the knowledge of God. We come to know Him primarily through effects, through creatures, as their First Cause, and from their perfection we affirm the Creator's perfection. But that is a very imperfect knowledge.

Afterward, we come to know Him better through faith, believing the One who knows God directly and who talked about Him, and who sealed His teaching with the glorious resurrection after death on the cross—Jesus Christ.

Finally, we most clearly come to know God directly, that is, after death—in heaven.

M. K.

79. IF GOD WERE TO CEASE TO EXIST... [1]

[Mugenzai no Seibo no Kishi, February 1935, pp. 2–3]

If God were to cease to exist, all of religion would lose its foundation. Religion is the relationship between God and man; if God did not exist, religion would lose its *raison d'être*, and prayer would cease to be necessary.

Justice would also disappear, because we would be limited to human judgment, but human judgment is not infallible. Even a man of good will can often be misled. Every day, how much injustice and arbitrariness we see in human judgments.

If God were to cease to exist—there would be nothing after death, so man's ultimate goal would only be this world.

Generally speaking, the ultimate goal is by its nature desired without any limitation, while other things are worthy desires only insofar as they are a means to achieving the ultimate goal. If this world were the ultimate goal, earthly riches would be desired without limitation; everyone would want to accumulate them as much as possible. As earthly riches are not unlimited, imperceptibly there would arise war among the people; everyone would want to acquire these riches. Consequently "the meat of the weaker would be the prey for today"—the stronger and the more clever would trample upon the others; people would use violence and, while living without any higher purpose, would be reduced to the status of an animal. Furthermore, if there was not a bit of forgiveness and compassion, it would be a wise law of life to fight with one's neighbor, to acquire the most riches and to use them as much as possible. If that happened, would not righteous people's lives be unbearable?

Yes: if God were to cease to exist—everything would lose its existence. If you ask "why?"—well, God not only created everything but also maintains everything, giving existence at every moment. Hence, if God were to cease to exist, along with Him, undoubtedly—the universe and all people would perish.

Yet God will not cease to exist, and so religion is not lost. God rewards or punishes even the smallest actions and thoughts, and He has for everyone glory or chastisement. Earthly riches are only a means to an eternal goal after death!

Korube

[1] If the proposition of the author—"if God were to cease to exist"—is not intended to be treated as absurd (God by His very nature cannot not exist, and therefore cannot cease to exist), one must obviously understand it as, "If God were to cease to exist...to me," in other words, "If I were to cease to acknowledge the existence of God..." - editor of the *Pisma*.

80. Faith

[Mugenzai no Seibo no Kishi, November 1935, pp. 2–3]

There are many interpretations on the subject of what religious faith is, and hence a clear explanation of its meaning is not without benefit.

Some explain faith as trust, others as some kind of religious feeling, and some give other interpretations.

However, in a few words, faith is the recognition of a truth heard externally, or learned about in some other way. For example, when somebody talks to me about a typhoon in a faraway country, or if I read about it or in some other way learn about the typhoon, and if I accept it as a true fact, then it is said that I have believed the speaker or the writer.

So, in an act of faith, there are two elements: recognition of the knowledge of the facts attesting to something, and recognition of this thing's truthfulness. Knowledge here means the mind's compliance in providing the man with the reality, whereas truthfulness means compliance of the testimony, spoken or written, with the mind, that is, with the testifier's knowledge.

This is true and applies to any act of faith, even in the context of the natural order, which has nothing to do with religious faith.

Religious faith is based on knowledge and truth, that is, on the Eternal Wisdom, who knows absolutely everything—and on His absolute perfect truthfulness, which not even once can oppose a single truth.

As a consequence of this, if we know something by way of reason to be divinely revealed, the authority of this revelation comes from the infinitely superior wisdom and truthfulness of God—and we recognize it as the truth on that basis. And this is a great act of faith.

In order that this act of recognition be made, special assistance from God is needed, assistance exceeding man's natural capacity. This special assistance is called divine grace.

Thus, the definition of religious faith is as follows: Faith is an act of reason that, at the command of the will moved by divine grace, recognizes a revealed truth.

Thus it is evident that it often happens that one studies religion for a long time, hears about it from many people, reads a great deal about it, deeply ponders and thinks about it, but does not ask God in humble prayer for the grace of faith and does not seek to humbly receive that grace—such a man will not make a single act of faith.

Korube

81. Prayer

[Mugenzai no Seibo no Kishi, June 1936, pp. 2–3]

Our contemporary fellow men, excessively engaged with material affairs, forget to pray. From morning to night—as if in a spell—they are preoccupied only with profit: whether at sea or on land, at the factory or at the shop.

Prayer is the expression of a beautiful soul. The human body was created from dust and after death will return to dust. All human activities also are returned to the earth. And only in time of prayer does man raise his heart to heaven and converse with the Creator of all things, and their First Cause, God.

Every good mother greatly rejoices when her child asks her for something. It is an expression of the child's confidence in his mother's goodness. In the same way, God joyfully recognizes our faith expressed to Him in prayer. This prayer does not have to be expressed in some rigidly established form. The essence of it is petition, thanksgiving, or adoration offered to God.

Whoever does not pray does not easily understand the spirit of prayer. Likewise, he cannot grasp the extent of the happiness that prayer offers the soul, or of the strength that prayer gives in everyday life.

God is well pleased with the prayer of those who are innocent, especially children.

In the autumn of last year, the famous Fr. Mateo [Crawley-Boevey, SS. CC.] from Peru, in South America, arrived in Japan and stayed for several months in Japan and Korea, preaching amidst his numerous trips throughout the country. I will cite the following example from his sermons.

In a church where Fr. Mateo was the confessor, there was a little girl who every time she received Holy Communion experienced a manifestation of Our Lord Jesus and spoke as a child with Him. One day, in order to make sure that it was really Our Lord Jesus who revealed Himself to her, Fr. Mateo said to her,

—Ask Our Lord Jesus for a gift.

—Yes of course, but for what gift?

—Say this to Our Lord Jesus: "My dear Jesus, my confessor instructed me to ask you for one soul, as proof that you are really Our Lord Jesus."

—Yes, I will do it willingly, but in regard to which soul? - asked the girl.

—You do not need to know that. Pray for the conversion of a soul that needs to be converted.

In the next confession, the girl told Fr. Mateo,

—Father, it has been fulfilled...

When he pretended that he did not believe her, the girl said,

—Father, have you forgotten that you told me that Our Lord Jesus must give proof? Our Lord Jesus said to me, "My little sister, I understand... Ask me for souls, I will willingly fulfill your desires... Tell Father that whenever he asks for souls, I will always hear him. And you, always be gentle and obedient, and strive always to love Me. For this you need to make sacrifices; however, do not do anything without your confessor's permission. I am more pleased with obedience than with sacrifice"; Our Lord Jesus said this. Father, the soul will come here shortly. Give me absolution quickly. Our Lord Jesus promised me that the soul will come during my confession.

When Fr. Mateo wanted to intercept these words and begin another conversation, the girl interrupted him:

—Father, I sense that the soul has come. Please give me absolution quickly!

The girl left the confessional and walked toward the altar to do her penance. When Fr. Mateo wished to leave, the door on the opposite side suddenly opened, and there appeared a man who was of high rank, but an atheist, and who had never knelt at his confessional. He said,

—Father, I do not know what has happened to me. Has grace overcome me? I do not have peace, I have come to confess.

And what a confession it was: this man, weeping, often repeated in the midst of the confession, "Why did this happen?" Fr. Mateo was able to point to that nice girl and say, "She has won you!"

At the moment of death, we will lose the right to any wealth we possess. Lest we sink amidst fleeting treasures, let us not forget to pray always in the evening before going to bed and in the morning after waking.

Korube

82. Our Ideal

[Mały Dziennik, June 24, 1936
Republished in RN 15 (1936) pp. 226–227]

Why has the *Small Daily* appeared on the journals' lists? Why have the *Knight* and the *Little Knight* captured more and more multitudes of souls? Why have so many brothers gathered at Niepokalanów and dedicated all their life to work [for the Immaculata], reducing their personal needs? Why have we traveled all the way to the "land of the cherry blossoms," and why do our aspirations embrace the entire world? What is our goal? What is our ideal?...

These and similar thoughts undoubtedly arise in the minds of men of good will.

I will forthrightly say that it is not easy to understand our ideal, and still more difficult to understand it in depth—rather, we can more and more deeply and clearly know it, but we will never fully reach its sublime depth. For what reason? The subject here concerns the Mother of God. We have an understanding of the notion of "mother," but the notion of "God" contains in itself the infinite, whereas our intelligence has limits. It will never be able, therefore, to grasp the concept of "Mother of God."

Thus, if a man cannot bend his knees and beg Her in humble prayer for the grace to know who She is, let him not expect to learn anything more intimate about Her.

From the divine Motherhood flow all the graces given to the Blessed Virgin Mary. The first of these is the Immaculate Conception. This privilege must be very dear to Her, if She willed to say of Herself at Lourdes, "I am the Immaculate Conception." By this name, dear to Her heart, we also wish to call Her.

The Immaculata—behold our ideal.

To come closer to Her, to become like Her, to let Her take possession of our heart and our whole being, so that She lives and acts in us and through us, so that She loves God with our heart, so that we belong to Her without limits—behold our ideal.

To radiate upon our surroundings, to win souls for Her, so that the hearts of our fellow men also may open before Her, so that She may reign in all men's hearts—wherever they are in the world, regardless of differences of race, nationality, or language—as well as in the hearts of all men who will ever be on earth until the end of the world—behold our ideal.

And that Her life would be deepened in us from day to day, from hour to hour, from moment to moment, and this without any limits—behold our ideal.

And that this Her life would similarly unfold in every soul that is and ever will be—behold our precious ideal.

Our Lord Jesus once said, in regard to understanding the sublime life of a virgin, "Who can understand, let him understand." And at the end of these few words I would like to add the same thing: "Who can understand, let him understand."

Unfortunately, even among those who have received holy baptism and perhaps have also deepened their religious knowledge, one still finds quite a lot of those who only with difficulty come to penetrate into the Heart of the Immaculata, the Mother of God, the Mother of Jesus our Brother, the Mother of our supernatural life, the Mediatrix of all graces, our Queen, Sovereign, Commander, and Dominator of Satan.

Fr. Maximilian M. Kolbe

83. MI [1]

[Rycerz Niepokalanej, December 1936, pp. 356–357]

On the cover of every issue of *Knight of the Immaculata*—the Polish, the Japanese, and the Italian—there is seen, on the left side of the figure of the Immaculata, a letter "M," and on the right an "I."

What do these letters mean?

"MI" is the international abbreviation of the name "Militia of the Immaculata," but in the Latin language, that is, *Militia Immaculatae*. The abbreviation is taken from the Latin language because it is the Church's language, and therefore in a way is supranational.

The abbreviation "MI" contains the entire essence of the Association of the Militia of the Immaculata.

The association is above all "I," that is, *Immaculatae*, or of the Immaculata. Every member's ideal—is to be of the Immaculata, to be Her servant, child, slave out of love, thing, and property, under any name that only love for Her has come up with, or will ever be able to think of. To be of Her: to be Hers in all respects and for life, death, and eternity. To be Hers without restrictions, irrevocably, forever. To become always more and more perfectly Hers, to become like Her, to unite oneself to Her, to become in a way Her, Herself, so that She may more and more rule over our soul, take possession of it totally, and in it and through it may She alone think, speak, and love God and neighbor, and—act. This is the ideal: to become Hers, of the Immaculata, *Immaculatae*—"I."

The one who becomes Hers in an increasingly perfect way will thereby also increasingly radiate upon his surroundings and encourage others to know the Immaculata ever more perfectly, to love Her more ardently, to come closer and closer to Her, and to give themselves to Her to the point of becoming totally—Her very self. Such a soul, the Immaculata's property, gains for Her more and more souls, and this by all legitimate means, and this soul becomes of the Immaculata—not only Her property but also a Knight, Lady, *Miles*—"M."

This is the meaning of the "M" and the "I," in the abbreviation "MI."

Let every glance at the cover of the *Knight of the Immaculata* remind us about this.

M. K.

[1] In fact, there was no title; rather, at the beginning of the text was printed a badge of the Militia of the Immaculata with the initials MI (*Militia Immaculatae*) and the standard of the association with the same initials, carried by an officer accompanied by a group of people of different states of life and paying homage to the Immaculata. - editor of the *Pisma*.

84. On the Second Day of July

[Rycerz Niepokalanej, July 1937, p. 193]

It is nearing two thousand years since the day when the Immaculate Virgin visited Her cousin Elizabeth, and on this day we celebrate the memory of this event. For the Most Holy Mother's visit lasts to the present day, and it occurs in every soul, and much more often than the individual soul imagines. Each and every grace, without exception, is the advent of the Mediatrix of all graces.

Do you want Her to see you often? Do you want Her to dwell permanently in your soul? Do you desire that She, and only She, direct your thoughts, that She take possession of all your heart? Do you desire to live totally for Her?

If you truly desire all this—open your heart to Her and give yourself to Her without limitation and forever, even if just with a sigh from your soul.

You can also help yourself with a formula, such as the act of consecration of the Militia of the Immaculata.

And have you ever thought of what you become when it is no longer you acting but She alone acting in you and through you, loving God and men?

Do you realize that when this is the case your actions are measured by Her dignity?

That in Her hands they become pure, unblemished, as She is utterly pure and immaculate?...

※ ※ ※

And is there something more that you could desire?

Rycerz Niepokalanej

85. What We Can Do

[Rycerz Niepokalanej, October 1937, pp. 292–293]

How many times have we heard the resigned or desperate expressions, "I cannot," "I cannot handle it," "I lack the strength."

Obviously, in the physical realm the strengths we have are limited, and it is pointless for someone to try to lift thousands of pounds with his hand.

In the moral realm, though, the same complaint can sometimes be heard: I cannot get rid of this fault, I do not have enough strength to acquire this virtue, it is beyond my strength.

Is it really true that we cannot?

After all, St. Paul expressly says, "I can do all"!... However, he also does not stop at that, but adds, "in Him who strengthens me." Only "without Me"—Our Lord Jesus Himself says—"you can do nothing."

Why?

Because if Almighty God asks something of us, it is certain that He will provide enough strength for us to accomplish His will, provided only that we do not neglect to do that which depends upon us.

We need divine grace to do good, and our soul can surely procure that grace through prayer.

We have an easy and sure way to possess all the grace we need. We have the Mediatrix of all graces. It is only necessary that we truly desire Her and thus keep away from Her less and less, that we love Her more heartily in temptations, difficulties, adversities, acknowledging Her power, Her universal mediation with God, and that we fly to Her with all confidence.

Then we too will be capable of everything, but in Him who strengthens us through the Immaculata.

Given below is the declaration from one of many souls that it is possible to do all through the Immaculata.

"Having been from a young age in a government job and among bad company, I forgot about family and my good education, and I was becoming day by day increasingly worse. Such a way of life had led me to complete moral corruption, and I had given myself to drunkenness. After some time I changed my environment and tried to start a new life, but even here I knew no peace. During this time I went to holy confession and devotions, but very rarely, and furthermore, out of habit. A few years later, having been persuaded, I subscribed to the *Knight of the Immaculata*, which I read almost mindlessly, and sometimes I was even in arrears of payment, even though I had enough for other expenses less necessary, and often even sumptuous and sinful. Living this way, I found myself at the bottom of moral ruin, and despite the voice of conscience, I did not turn back from this path.

"A few years later I encountered the tremendous consequences and effects of this miserable way of living, along with scarcity and misery, and I was close to losing my job. These misfortunes completely took away all my desire to live. There came a time when my life was hanging by a thread, and a storm of despairing and suicidal thoughts raged around me.

"Being in so pitiful a state, totally abandoned by men, derided by them and covered in the mud of human words, I was sitting in my apartment browsing through the old issues of the monthly *Knight* magazine, and it was as if a new life began to awake in me. Having not completely lost the good that my mother taught me, and reading the *Knight of the Immaculata*, in particular—thank you—I thought that I could still pray to the Blessed Virgin Mary, who does not despise anyone. Perhaps I could still receive the grace of conversion and deliverance from my life's misfortunes. I decided to attend the May devotions and to pray a novena to St. Thérèse of the Child Jesus.

"After a certain period of time, I felt a blissful peace and began a new life, and this grace I decided to publicly announce.

"And so I was not disappointed in having placed my confidence therein, because this Blessed Virgin Mary and St. Thérèse gave back to me peace of mind and health and reduced the crosses in my life. (An unworthy servant of Mary, A., clerk)."

If you are already dropping your hands, try to benefit from this truth, and you will be convinced that you also can do all things through the Immaculata.

R. N.

86. The Lord Is Truly Risen!

[Echo Niepokalanowa, 16 IV 1938]

It is springtime. Leaves are budding, and near the statue of the Immaculata the peach tree is in full bloom.

With this background, we hear the joyful hymns of the feast of the resurrection, which according to the words of St. Paul forms the foundation of our faith in Our Lord Jesus.

"Christ is risen"—repeated by thousands of mouths on this day.

"We also must rise again," the Easter hymn proclaims to us, but not only after death—every year Holy Church urges the faithful to do this by commanding the Easter confession.

We friars even more must rise from the dead. Even if one had the misfortune to die spiritually, even if Satan told him that he would never again rise from the dead, it is enough to sincerely turn to the Mediatrix of all graces—the Immaculata—to not only obtain the grace of resurrection but also reach a high, very high degree of sanctity.

The more one approaches Her, the more abundantly one draws from the graces of knowledge and a generous love of God, who for love of us went even to the cross.

Br. Maximilian M.,
guardian

87. Where Are We Going?

[Echo Niepokalanowa, 30 IV 1938]

To the Divine Heart of Jesus through the Immaculata—is our watchword. Through the Immaculata—is our essential character. As an instrument in Her hand... Hence, it is not enough for us to try to be in every respect ever more belonging to the Immaculata within some defined limit, but we wish to radiate Her, in order to draw to Her the souls of others, indeed all who are, will be, and could be, without limitation—in a word, we are to become more and more Hers, even knights, ready to sacrifice self entirely for Her, to the last drop of blood, in the conquest of the whole world and every soul in particular for Her, and that as quickly as possible, as quickly as possible, as quickly as possible—MI.

And let each one of us say: this ideal I desire to fully implement and realize ever more, and more quickly in myself. I must strive to be more and more of the Immaculata. I am just myself; I must give myself more and more to Her, make myself similar to Her, live for Her, radiate Her, so that my surroundings are illuminated more clearly with the knowledge of Her and ever more ardently inspired and inflamed with love for Her, so that others will more and more become like me, as I am like Her, and so through me they may become more Hers, so that they radiate more and more, as I do, and enlighten and ignite more and more of their fellow men—so that the whole world and every soul may become more and more Hers, almost Her, Herself—MI—me.

What means do I use? Any, as long as it is licit. One powerful means is the binding together of individual forces, of individual souls. Hence the Association of the Militia of the Immaculata.

Where there is the joining of forces there is the need for one head; hence the headquarters, Niepokalanów.

And this headquarters is trying to help the members of Niepokalanów to achieve the MI's goal (<u>MIN</u>), and our fellow countrymen (<u>MIP</u>), and all others through <u>MIM</u>, or MI *mundialis*—the world.

Br. Maximilian M.,
guardian

 **About Leonine Publishers**

Leonine Publishers LLC makes fine Catholic literature available to Catholics throughout the English-speaking world. Leonine Publishers offers an innovative "hybrid" approach to book publication that helps authors as well as readers. Please visit our web site at www.leoninepublishers.com to learn more about us. Browse our online bookstore to find more solid Catholic titles to uplift, challenge, and inspire.

Our patron and namesake is Pope Leo XIII, a prudent, yet uncompromising pope during the stormy years at the close of the 19th century. Please join us as we ask his intercession for our family of readers and authors.

Do you have a book inside you? Visit our web site today. Leonine Publishers accepts manuscripts from Catholic authors like you. If your book is selected for publication, you will have an active part in the production process. This book is an example of our growing selection of literature for the busy Catholic reader of the 21st century.

www.leoninepublishers.com

www.ingramcontent.com/pod-product-compliance
Lightning Source LLC
LaVergne TN
LVHW011419080426
835512LV00005B/155